DISCARD

CIVILIZATIONS OF THE AMERICAS

Native American cultures of North, Central and South America

Devised and produced by Andrea Dué
Text by Renzo Rossi and Martina Veutro

MACMILLAN LIBRARY REFERENCE USA
NEW YORK

INTRODUCTION

First published in Italian by Jaca Book
© Editoriale Jaca Book Spa, Milano,
1995

This edition published 1996
by Macmillan Library Reference USA
1633 Broadway, 5th Floor,
New York, NY 10019

English Language Translation
Copyright © Simon and Schuster
Macmillan 1996

Devised and produced by Andrea Dué
Text by Renzo Rossi and Martina Veutro
Scientific consultant Giuseppe Orefici
Translation by Patricia Borlenghi
Edited by Andrea Dué and Martina
Veutro
American edition edited by Brian
Williams
Color illustrations by Giorgio Bacchin,
Alessandro Baldanzi, Lorenzo Cecchi,
Lorenzo Pieri, Paola Ravaglia,
Alessandro Bartolozzi, Roberto Simoni
Black and white illustrations by
Alessandro Baldanzi, Roberto Simoni
Design by Andrea Dué

Library of Congress Cataloging-in-
Publication Data

Rossi, Renzo 1940–
  [Atlanti della storia dell'uomo.
English]
  The atlas of human history/devised and
produced by Andrea Dué; text by Renzo
Rossi.
    p.; cm.
  Includes indexes.
  Contents: [1] The first people – [2]
The first settlers – [3] Cradles of
civilization – [4] The first Europeans –
[5] Civilizations of Asia – [6]
Civilizations of the Americas.
  ISBN 0-02-860285-4 (v. 1). –
  ISBN 0-02-860286-2 (v. 2). –
  ISBN 0-02-860287-0 (v. 3). –
  ISBN 0-02-860288-9 (v. 4). –
  ISBN 0-02-860289-7 (v. 5). –
  ISBN 0-02-860290-0 (v. 6). –
  1. History, Ancient – Maps for
children. 2. Historical geography –
Maps for children. 3. Children's atlases.
[1. Civilization, Ancient – Maps.
2. Historical geography – Maps.
3. Atlases.]
  I. Dué, Andrea. II. Title.
G1033.R6 1996 <G&M>
930–dc20   95-8622
                                 CIP
                              MAP AC

Printed and bound in Italy by Grafiche
Editoriali Padane Spa, Cremona

The first peoples of the Americas had their roots in prehistoric East Asia. We do not know exactly when or how people first migrated from the Old World to the New World. It must have been during the last Ice Age, when Asia and North America were connected by a strip of land. Across this bridge, people from East Asia were able to travel to new lands in a continent where no people had ever dwelt before.

This volume of THE ATLAS OF HUMAN HISTORY guides you through the early stages of the settlement by human beings of the Americas, and the rise of the first civilizations there. The early settlers made their homes in the continent's frozen sub-Arctic lands, along the coasts and river valleys, and in the dry lands of the southwest. They settled in the forests and woodlands of the east coast, and on the great plains that covered much of the interior. They lived as hunters, fishers and farmers in harmony with the wilderness. Moving through the narrow isthmus of Central America, they travelled into the tropical forests, mountains and grasslands of South America.

The maps and reconstructions in *Civilizations of the Americas* illustrate important stages in this long process, and the different kinds of cultures that were developed – from the hunters of the Arctic to the temple and pyramid builders of Mexico. In places impressive monuments still stand, the ruins of great cities and religious centres. But there are mysteries still unsolved, for many early American cultures have vanished into legend, or have been absorbed or destroyed by other cultures, more powerful and more aggressive.

Humans in America developed an innate sense of the spirit of nature. People believed that divine forces were at work in sunlight, birth and death, as well as everyday activities such as farming, war and trade. The gods who were all around were able to intervene in human affairs. Much Early American art celebrated the gods, and the powerful beliefs founded in these ideas lasted for hundreds of years. This religious tradition provides the bedrock of a Native American spiritual heritage. It exerts its power today, even in the modern world with all its technologies, where the Native American is the longest-rooted migrant among so many settlers in a New World.

B. W.

CONTENTS

1 THE PEOPLING OF AMERICA

NORTH
AMERICA

Inuit (Eskimos) 14,000

ASIA

Paleo-Indians 40,000 – 15,000   ○ Dry Creek (11,000)
                                  ○ Tangle Lakes (12,000)

Proto-Aleuts 14,000 – 8,500   Na-Dene

GREENLAND

Davis
Strait

LABRADOR

Baffin
Bay

SEA

Canadian
Arctic
Islands

Devon I.

Baffin Island

Hudson Strait

Queen

Labrador
Peninsula

Elizabeth

Islands   Somerset Island

Prince Patrick
Island

Melville
Island

Prince of
Wales Island

Southampton Island

Banks Island

Victoria
Island

Hudson
Bay

Wrangel Island

Beaufort
Sea

Great Bear
Lake

Siberia

Great Slave
Lake

L. Winnipeg

Bering Strait

Seward
Peninsula

ALASKA

Yukon

GREAT   PLAINS

ROCKY   MOUNTAINS

Sheaman
(Wyoming)

Gulf
of
Alaska

Anzick Cache
(Montana)   Lindenmeier (C

Colby
Wyoming)

Kodiak Island

Queen
Charlotte
Island

Mammoth Ki
Wyomin

Alaskan Peninsula

Vancouver
Island

Richey-Roberts Clovis Cache
(Washington)

Simon Cache
(Idaho)

Wilson Butte
(Idaho)

Dietz
(Oregon)

PACIFIC

OCEAN

Arizo

This arrowhead was made by
people of the Folsom culture, a
name that comes from a site in
New Mexico where prehistoric
tools about 10,000 years old have
been discovered. Such finds
convinced scientists that people
arrived in America earlier than was
once thought.

Old Crow (27000)
Bluefish Cave (13000)
Dry Creek (11000)
Taber (40000)
Minnesota (10000)
Meadowcroft Shelter (1900-14000)
La Jolla (21500)
Santa Rosa Is. (30000)
Midland (8600)
Astahuacan (9000)
Chicoloapan (7000)
Tlaoacoia (22000)
Muaco (14250)
Punin (10000)
Pikimachay (22000)
Pedra Furada (32000)

Far left: This small map shows the land bridge that joined Asia and North America during the last Ice Age. The red arrows show probable routes, with dates (years ago) as the ancestors of the Inuit moved north, the Aleuts journeyed south to the Aleutian Islands, and the Na-Dené made their homes along the Gulf of Alaska. The symbols ○ mark known sites.

Left: People moved south, eventually reaching South America. Shading indicates the main areas of settlement. Symbols ○ with dates mark known sites.

The main map shows sites ▲ settled by the Paleo-Indians, the first inhabitants of North America. These people were hunters and their stone tools and weapons have been found.

Newfoundland

Anticosti Island

Nova Scotia

Debert

St. Lawrence

L. Ontario

Shawnee-Minisink (Pennsylvania)

Shoop (Pennsylvania)

Thunderbird (Virginia)

L. Huron

L. Erie

Williamson (Virginia)

Meadowcroft (Pennsylvania)

L. Michigan

Ohio

APPALACHIAN ALPS

Kimmswick (Missouri)

Wells Creek (Tennessee)

Mississippi

Domebo (Oklahoma)

Miami (Texas)

Folsom (New Mexico)

Clovis (New Mexico)

Levi (Texas)

Mockingbird Gap (New Mexico)

Windward Islands

Puerto Rico

Trinidad

Haiti

Bahamas

Florida

Cuba

Jamaica

CARIBBEAN SEA

SOUTH AMERICA

GULF
OF
MEXICO

Yucatán Peninsula

Central America

Isthmus of Panama

PACIFIC

OCEAN

SIERRA MADRE ORIENTAL

SIERRA MADRE OCCIDENTAL

Gulf of California

Baja California Peninsula

1 THE PEOPLING OF AMERICA

The small maps (right) show the migration routes and main cultures of prehistoric America. The tools shown are (top) a Paleo-Indian two-sided point and (below) a Clovis point.

LOWER OLD STONE AGE

UPPER OLD STONE AGE

MIDDLE STONE AGE

NEW STONE AGE

It is clear that modern people, *Homo sapiens sapiens*, reached the American continent from the Old World in the late Pleistocene epoch during the last Ice Age – from 80,000 to 9,000 years ago. In North America this period of glaciation is called Wisconsin. In Eurasia, it is known as the Wurm glaciation.

A layer of ice up to three kilometres (nearly two miles) thick stretched as far south as the Ohio and Mississippi rivers, covering what are now the Great Plains. Frozen tundra eventually gave way to forest, and further south in Mexico there were probably prairies. Ice and snow persisted on the mountains of the Central American sierras and the Andes of South America.

Across the land bridge

The first groups of hunters reached Alaska and the Yukon valley. These people came from eastern Siberia and were able to travel through areas that were ice-free. They crossed what is now the Bering Strait by a strip of land some 1,600 kilometres (about a thousand miles) wide that had emerged from the sea as ocean levels dropped during the Ice Age.

When this bridge-crossing happened is still unclear. Evidence is contradictory. Some experts, using radiocarbon techniques to date sites and primitive stone tools, put the arrival of people in America at 20,000 years ago, or earlier. Others take the starting point to be the first fully attested Paleo-Indian culture, known as Clovis – not much before 12,000 years ago.

Dating the first Americans

Studying the types of stone tools used by these first Americans, experts have proposed three divisions of the Old Stone Age – Lower, Middle and Upper.

The Old Crow Basin site in the northern Yukon (northwest Canada) has revealed broken and hand-worked mammal bones from the Pleistocene, as well as some stone tools dated to between 29,100 and 25,750 years old. More certain dates for human settlement in the Lower Old Stone Age before the Clovis culture come from the Meadowcroft Rockshelter site south of Pittsburgh, Pennsylvania. In an ice-free area of the Appalachian tableland, carbonized fragments of materials have been found. The fragments were worked by humans and analysis by the carbon-14 method dates the finds earlier than 17,000 years ago. The most recent layers, from 14,000 to 10,900 years ago, yielded stone tools shaped with edges on one or two sides: knives, engraving tools and a two-edged spearpoint.

Other evidence from the Lower Old Stone Age comes from Wilson Butte Cave in Idaho, where bones and stone tools from 14,500 to 15,000 years ago have been found. Similar finds come from the Levi Rockshelter in Texas, and from temporary settlement sites used by wandering hunters, found in the state of Puebla in Mexico. There are interesting but controversial finds from the Pikimachay Cave in Peru and from Monte Verde in Chile, a village that existed 13,500 to 12,500 years ago. Brazil has provided theoretical evidence of even older settlement, varying from 40,000 to 20,000 years ago.

Clovis and Folsom toolmakers

The Clovis and Folsom cultures of the Middle Old Stone Age have left undoubted evidence. Most widespread was the Clovis culture, named after the Blackwater Draw site near Clovis in New Mexico. This culture started around 12,000 years ago and lasted for 800 years. The most northerly site is that of Debert in Nova Scotia, Canada. But the Clovis culture spread throughout the western United States, and as far south as Mexico, Guatemala, Costa Rica and Panama.

Small bands of Clovis people hunted mammoths, horses, bison, tapirs, camel-like mammals, and caribou. The

These digging tools (1, 2) were probably used for grubbing up roots or flints for toolmaking. Scrapers like these (3, 5, 6) were used by Paleo-Indians for preparing animal skins. Small chips of stone (4) were thrown away by toolmakers, who chipped away at the edges of blades to make a sharp cutting or scraping edge (7, 8).

The map (right) shows the main Native American groups before European settlement began. The two tools are Folsom points.

This rush duck (right) was used as a hunting decoy.

ambushed the animals, chasing them into bogs or over cliffs, and then killed them with stone-tipped spears. The speartip known as the Clovis point has no equivalent in the Old World, and the spear fixed to it was flung with the aid of a spearthrower. Clovis people also spent much of their time gathering plant foods.

In 1926 scientists from the Museum of Natural History in Denver discovered at Folsom, New Mexico, bones belonging to the extinct long-horned bison. They also found stone tools, among which was a spearhead chiselled on both sides and with grooves. This point, based on the Clovis one, is the typical tool of the people called Folsom, after it. At a camp site in Lindenmeier, Colorado, scrapers, knives, awls, needles and bone engraving tools dating from 10,800 years ago have been found.

Hunters on the move

There is other evidence to show that by this time people were well established in America, and making objects from minerals such as silica and jasper. By 7,000 years ago, more advanced cultures had succeeded Clovis and Folsom. Their people were able to survive the changes brought about by climatic variation, and the extinction of some of the prehistoric animals hunted by earlier peoples.

By 9,000 years ago, there were stone-toolmakers in Mexico, and analysis of wood carbon from fire remains at Fell's Cave in Patagonia (South America) shows that humans were living here, too, about 11,000 years ago – at roughly the same time as the Clovis culture. Tools made from basalt, flint and quartz have been found in these sites. The people who made them hunted horses and giant ground-sloths. It is clear that people moved through America with surprising speed, hunting its abundant wild animals. Between 14,000 and 7,000 years ago, hunters also moved into the cold northern Arctic lands, as the Wisconsin ice sheet retreated.

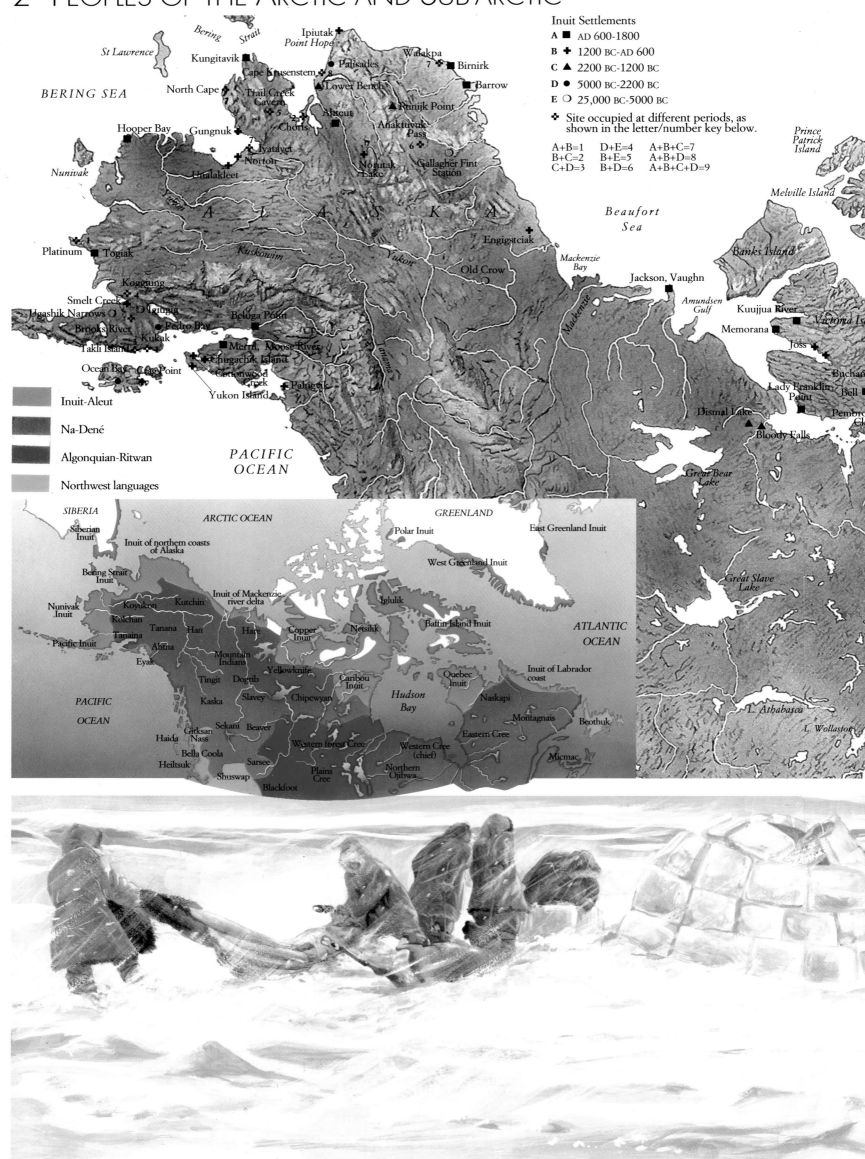

Bering Strait

St Lawrence

Ipiutak
Point Hope

Walakpa
7   Birnirk

Kungitavik

Cape Krusenstern   8   Palisades
Barrow

BERING SEA   North Cape   Trail Creek   Lower Bench
Cavern   5   Ahteut   Punjik Point

Choris   2   Anaktuvuk
Pass

Hooper Bay   Gungnuk   Iyatayet   7   6
Norton   Nunamiut   Gallagher Flint
Lake   Station

Nunivak   Unalakleet

Yukon

Platinum   Togiak   Kuskowim

Koggiung   Old Crow

Smelt Creek   Igiugig
Ugashik Narrows   Beluga Point
Brooks River   Pedro Bay
Takli Island   Kukak
Merrill, Moose River
Ocean Bay   Crag Point   Chugachik Island
Yukon Island   Cottonwood
Creek   Palugvik

PACIFIC
OCEAN

Inuit Settlements

A ■ AD 600–1800
B ✚ 1200 BC–AD 600
C ▲ 2200 BC–1200 BC
D ● 5000 BC–2200 BC
E ○ 25,000 BC–5000 BC
✚ Site occupied at different periods, as shown in the letter/number key below.

A+B=1   D+E=4   A+B+C=7
B+C=2   B+E=5   A+B+D=8
C+D=3   B+D=6   A+B+C+D=9

Prince
Patrick
Island

Melville Island

Banks Island

Beaufort
Sea

Mackenzie
Bay

Jackson, Vaughn

Amundsen
Gulf   Kuujjua River

Memorana   Victoria Is
Joss

Lady Franklin
Point   Bell
Buchan

Dismal Lake   Pembro
Cla

Bloody Falls

Great Bear
Lake

Mackenzie

Legend
- Inuit-Aleut
- Na-Dené
- Algonquian-Ritwan
- Northwest languages

SIBERIA   ARCTIC OCEAN   GREENLAND

Siberian
Inuit   Polar Inuit   East Greenland Inuit

Inuit of northern coasts
of Alaska   West Greenland Inuit

Bering Strait
Inuit   Iglulik

Nunivak
Inuit   Koyukon   Kutchin   Inuit of Mackenzie
river delta   Netsilik   Baffin Island Inuit   ATLANTIC
OCEAN

Pacific Inuit   Kolchan   Hare   Copper
Inuit
Tanana   Han   Inuit
Tanaina   Ahtna   Mountain   Quebec
Eyak   Indians   Inuit   Inuit of Labrador
coast

PACIFIC   Tingit   Dogrib   Yellowknife   Caribou
Inuit
OCEAN   Kaska   Slavey   Hudson   Naskapi
Chipewyan   Bay   Great Slave
Lake

Sekani   Beaver   Montagnais   Beothuk
Haida   Gitksan
Nass   Eastern Cree   L. Athabasca
Bella Coola   Western forest Cree
Heiltsuk   Sarsee   Western Cree
(chief)   Micmac   L. Wollaston
Shuswap   Plains   Northern
Blackfoot   Cree   Ojibwa

ATLANTIC OCEAN

The large map shows archaeological sites in the Arctic, and their approximate dates. The small map (far left) shows the four cultural areas of the Arctic and the peoples who lived in them.

Queen
Elizabeth
Islands

Ellesmere

Tumstone Beach

Inglefield Land

Aanartoq — Inuarfissuaq, Ruin Island, Cape Russel, Cape Kent

Old Nuuliit

Thule

Illummersuit

GREENLAND

Port Refuge

Dundas Island

Devon Is.

Craig Harbour

1 Resolute

Maxwell Bay

Somerset Island

Nanguvik

7

Mittimatalik

Inussuk

Saqqaq

7 Sermermiut

Ammassalik

Prince of Wales Is.

Strathcona Sound

Qilalukan

Baffin Bay

Itinnera

Channel

Boothia Peninsula

Gulf of Boothia

Baffin Land

Parry Hill

Igloolik

King William Is.

Malerualik

Pingitkalik

Prince Charles Island

Melville Peninsula

L. Nettilling

L. Amadjuak

Cumberland Sound

Kangek

Ilutalik

Davis Strait

Naujan

Foxe Channel

Shaymark

Crystall II

Closure

Silumjut

Southampton Island

Ighiligardjuk

Coats

Hudson

Strait

Tyara

Ungava Peninsula

Diana Bay

Imaha

Ungava Bay

Saglek Bay

Labrador Sea

ATLANTIC OCEAN

Hudson Bay

Mansel

Labrador Peninsula

Seahorse Gully

9

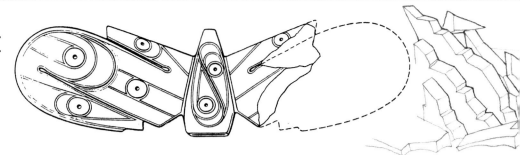

The Arctic region is the northernmost area of the world. The part in America shows evidence of humans from 5000 BC, but may have been inhabited as long as 18,000 years ago. A series of so-called *akmak* tools, found on the annual caribou migration route at the site of Onion Portage, suggests that people lived here at least 10,000 years ago.

The peoples of the Arctic were once considered a separate ethnic group from other Native Americans. But like the Paleo-Indians, they too came from Asia and their features, particularly the shape of their eyes, suggest links with the Mongoloid peoples of the Bering Sea coasts.

Two groups evolved from these Asian migrants: the Aleuts who settled in the Aleutian Islands of the north Pacific, and the Inuit (also known as Eskimos) who settled in Alaska, the Canadian Arctic and in western Greenland. A second migration from Siberia took place around 4,000 years ago. From 3,000 to 1,000 years ago people known as Ipiutak arrived, and settled mainly on the coasts. Traces of them remain on the Point Hope site. The direct ancestors of the modern Inuit were the Thule, who settled later, around AD 1100.

The Inuit

Inuit society was organized around two basic activities: fishing and hunting. Along the coasts, the main sources of food were seal, walrus and whale. Inland, the Inuit hunted caribou and musk ox. The skins of these animals, with fur from polar bears and Arctic foxes, were used to make warm jackets and trousers to protect their wearers from the bitter cold of winter.

The Inuits' ice shelters, or igloos, were made comfort-

This piece of ivory (above) was a stabilizer fin, fixed to a spear. It worked like the feathered flight of an arrow.

This reconstruction (right) is of an Inuit hut from Barrow, Alaska, which was ice-covered for 500 years. Here there were some trees, so people could use timber for building. The hut was partly buried by snow in winter. It had two floors, and served as home, storehouse and workshop. The fireplace was on the ground floor, heat and smoke rising to warm the upper rooms.

able inside by covering the walls with layers of furs and skins. The opening was a tunnel built low down, so that the wind was kept out and as little warmth as possible was lost from the family living space. In summer, people lived in tents made from seal or caribou skin.

The magic of the shaman

The most important person in the Inuit community was the shaman, who was believed to have mystic powers that allowed him to contact the spirit world. Shamans were believed to be capable of curing sickness, and of influencing the success or failure of hunting and fishing. If a person broke a taboo, or tribal law, the shaman had the power to restore harmony between people and the universe. During the Arctic winters, the shaman presided over feasts, usually with dancing and rites to please the spirits.

The scene below (pictured in colour on pages 8/9) shows Inuit life in the freezing Arctic winter. Snow-houses called igloos provided either a temporary shelter for hunters or a more permanent family home. Along the coast Inuit hunted seals, walruses and whales, from skin boats. These animals provided meat to eat, oil for lamps, and skins for clothing and bedding. People living inland hunted polar bears, caribou and musk ox, sometimes using traps.

Inside the snow house, sheltered from the wind, the people were warm, and could enjoy their meal. Groups of igloos were sometimes linked by tunnels, so that people could visit each other without enduring the howling winds outside.

Even so, it was a tough life, with little or no vegetation and long winter weeks of near-total darkness. To enliven their somewhat monotonous diet, Inuit people caught fish and sea birds, using either bows, or the bolas as a throwing weapon. They preserved meat and fish by smoking or drying, and by storing them in ice.

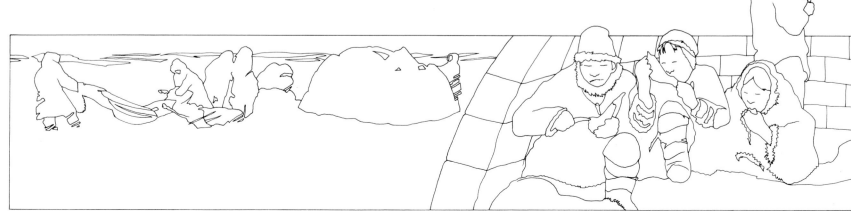

Tundra and forest dwellers

South of the Arctic were large regions of treeless tundra, beyond which stretched vast forests. Here the climate was less harsh. First settled by Paleo-Indians, these areas were occupied by various groups of hunters and fishers. To the east and south were the proto-Algonquin, and to the west were the Athabascans, named after the Canadian lake Athabasca.

None of these peoples practised farming. But because their environment was more varied than that of the snowy Arctic, with a greater variety of plants and animals, they had more foods to choose from. They hunted caribou, bison, musk ox, moose, bear, porcupine, rabbit and other smaller animals. In the rivers they caught salmon. Finding food was their basic activity, and there was little in the way of social life. The different tribal groups kept to themselves, each having its own territory for hunting and fishing.

Clothing, ornaments and society

Clothing was made from animal skins. It was decorated with flower-patterns, fringes, porcupine quills and animal tails. Women often tattooed their faces. Men wore feathers in their hair and painted their faces with bright colours. They made necklaces and amulets from shells, and also pierced their noses to wear shell decorations.

Some tribes had two classes of people: nobles and workers, with (more rarely) a third and lowest rank of slaves. Wars between tribes were fought with knives, spears and bows and arrows. Most tools were made from wood, horn or bone. Stone tools were less common.

For the Indians of the sub-Arctic lands, the shaman was a mystic contact with the supernatural world. The shaman had authority over other members of the tribe, but in the absence of a shaman, ordinary people could contact the spirits too. They might do this during a dream or trance, a state of being in which people could re-establish the magical link with the unseen forces of the universe.

Some essential tools (above). The wooden tool (1) has seal claws fixed to one end, and was used by a seal-hunter to rake the ice from around a seal's breathing hole. The wood and bone pick (2) was used for clearing snow from the igloo entrance. The bolas (3) made from seal bone and thongs was hurled at sea birds.

These red-painted copper plates (below) are in the shape of shields. They were worn as marks of social rank by people living around the Skeena river in British Columbia, Canada.

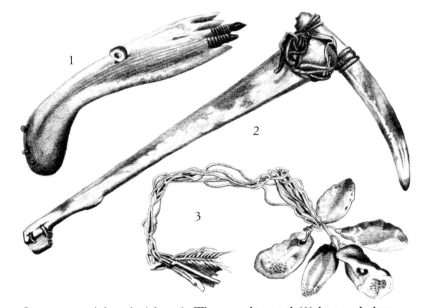

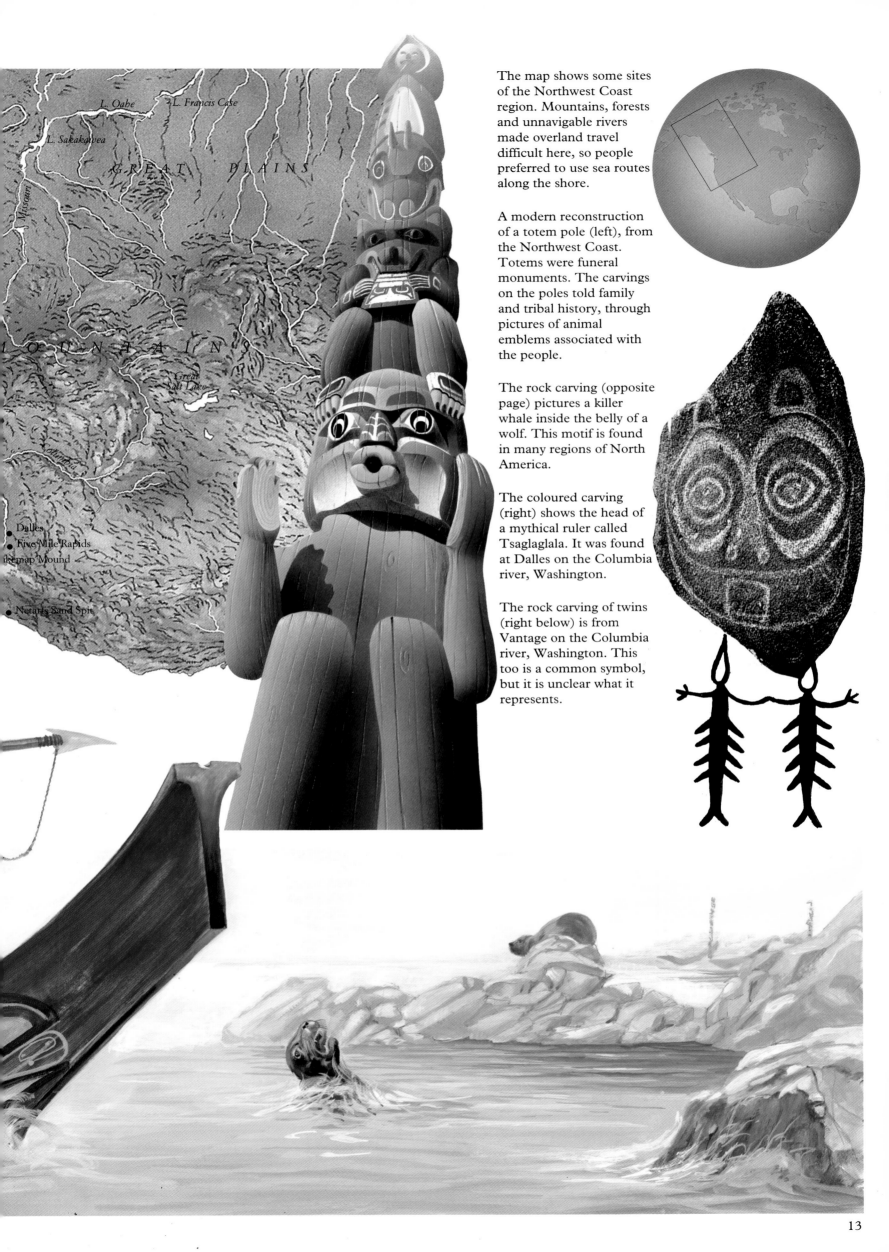

The map shows some sites of the Northwest Coast region. Mountains, forests and unnavigable rivers made overland travel difficult here, so people preferred to use sea routes along the shore.

A modern reconstruction of a totem pole (left), from the Northwest Coast. Totems were funeral monuments. The carvings on the poles told family and tribal history, through pictures of animal emblems associated with the people.

The rock carving (opposite page) pictures a killer whale inside the belly of a wolf. This motif is found in many regions of North America.

The coloured carving (right) shows the head of a mythical ruler called Tsaglaglala. It was found at Dalles on the Columbia river, Washington.

The rock carving of twins (right below) is from Vantage on the Columbia river, Washington. This too is a common symbol, but it is unclear what it represents.

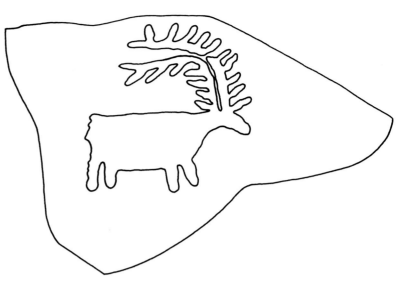

This rock carving of a moose (above) was found near the Columbia river.

The long west coast of North America is a good place for people to live, partly because the warm ocean current flowing east across the Pacific Ocean keeps the climate gentle. In the north, from the tip of Alaska up to the border of California, there are many small islands, tongues of land, and inlets of the sea along a coastal strip sheltered by mountains. The only large rivers flowing from the interior to the sea are the Fraser and Columbia, both rich in salmon. The heavy rains water thick forests.

Because of its geographic isolation, the region remained uninhabited until Paleo-Indians reached it around 11,000 to 8,000 years ago. These people were hunter-gatherers who gradually adapted to coastal life, collecting shellfish and catching fish and marine animals. The rich food resources of the sea, exploited more and more by these peoples, made this region a Land of Plenty.

Although the settlers did not become farmers until much later, they achieved a comfortable standard of living. Their self-sufficiency meant that they had no need to trade, and they produced a surplus of goods themselves. This had a curious and unique result.

Giving it away

Wealth, and symbols of wealth, became very important in Northwest society. Highly sought-after were the elaborate goods made by craftworkers, such as blankets, baskets and fine carved wooden objects. These goods became articles of exchange, used to purchase slaves or the exclusive right to a name or even a song, which no other person was allowed to use.

This economic system produced a ceremony known as *potlatch*, which took the form of a giving-away party. Members of a community gave away a large part of their property, as a sign of their prestige. The more the giver handed out to his neighbours, the higher his prestige. The wealth lost was later regained in other ceremonies, in which the giver joined those receiving gifts from another generous party-giver.

California culture

The culture of the southern coastal peoples, in California, had some common characteristics. But here the landscape and climate were more diverse, leading to greater differences between groups. They shared the ancient hunting, fishing and food-gathering way of life, but developed their own social patterns.

Californian society was simple and remained little changed

The scene below (in colour on pages 12/13) shows people of the Northwest coast hunting seal. The men are using a canoe which has been hollowed out from a red cedar trunk, first with fire, burning away the core, and then with axes and chisels. The canoe has a high prow, decorated and carved. The picture of a killer whale on the canoe is a magical emblem designed to protect the hunters.

The men are using pointed wooden paddles, which can also be used as weapons. The harpooner is the leader of the band. He wears a carved wooden club in his belt, as a sign of his authority.

The hunters are poised for success as the harpooner prepares to strike at a seal in the water. He has a harpoon made of yew wood, tipped with shell or bone. The line is attached to an inflated sealskin float, which prevents the prey from diving to escape.

This strange cup (below) is made of steatite, or soapstone, and probably belonged to a shaman. It comes from the Fraser Valley, and is about a thousand years old.

This carving of a killer whale (above) is from Ozette in Canada. The animal, a feared hunter of the sea, was a symbol of power.

for some 4,000 years until relatively modern times. The people seem never to have felt the need to begin farming or trading, but this did not hinder their expansion to the point where there were at least 500 different tribes.

Mountain and desert cultures

The people living in the mountains and deserts of the West developed their own cultures, influenced by contacts with peoples in the forests of the East. The people of the West lived in what are now Idaho, northeastern Oregon, eastern Washington, Nevada, Utah and the Rocky Mountains. From 6000 to 2500 BC the climate became drier, and many people faced hardships as deserts spread. They adapted by seeking new food supplies, gathering berries and roots as well as hunting.

These people borrowed from the East the custom of burying the dead beneath burial mounds, although the mounds themselves were not so large. They built their homes partly underground, covering them with roofs made from reeds and tree bark. They made pictures on rocks, carving or hammering designs that are still visible. They also made woven baskets. Evidence for these comes from Danger Cave in western Utah. The baskets were made watertight, and were in fact used to carry water, since these people had no pottery.

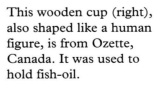

This armour made of strips of wood was worn over a tunic to protect the chest. It was used by warriors from the Kwakiutl tribe of the Northwest. Helmets were also made of wood.

This wooden cup (right), also shaped like a human figure, is from Ozette, Canada. It was used to hold fish-oil.

4 ADENA, HOPEWELL AND MISSISSIPPI CULTURES

The two maps below show the regions in which the Adena and Hopewell (left) and Mississippi (right) cultures were strongest. The Adena culture developed along the middle course of the Ohio river. Its trade links were wide, and attracted people from faraway areas. But by the 5th century BC the Adenas were in decline, replaced by the Hopewells in the lower Ohio valley, along which Hopewell culture was spread. The middle course of the Mississippi river was the area from which Mississippi culture spread, after about 800 BC. The culture known as 'Fort Ancient', along the middle course of the Ohio, derived from the Hopewell.

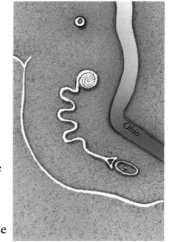

This ceremonial spoked wheel (right) the High Plains was marked out on the ground. The main spoke points toward the sun at dawn in midsummer.

▨	burial mounds
▨	Hopewell complexes
▨	Hopewell-Adena centres

This earth burial mound (right) in the form of a snake was made by the Adena people of Ohio. Known as the Great Serpent Mound, it is 400 metres (a quarter of a mile) long from nose to tail, not counting the coils.

▨	Oneota culture
▨	Middle Mississippian culture
▨	Mississippi-Caddo culture
▨	Plaquemine-Mississippi culture
▨	Appalachian-Mississippian culture
▨	Fort Ancient culture

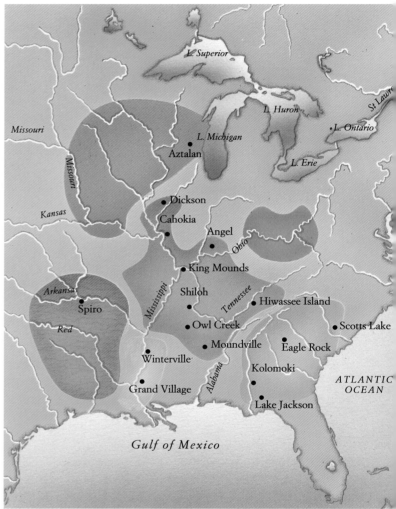

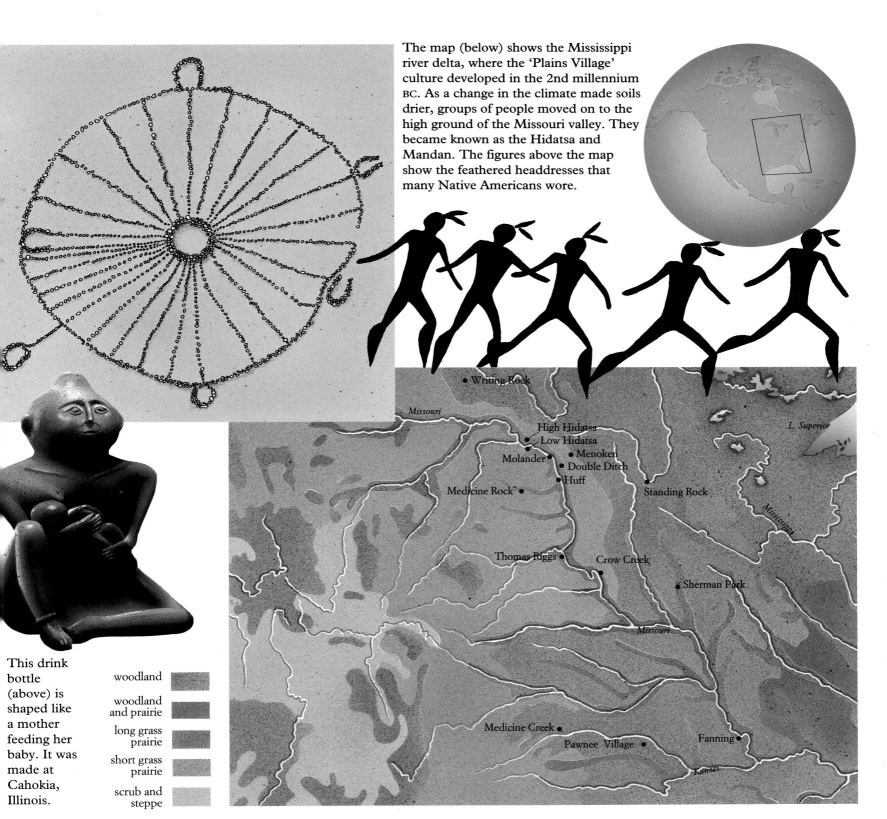

The map (below) shows the Mississippi river delta, where the 'Plains Village' culture developed in the 2nd millennium BC. As a change in the climate made soils drier, groups of people moved on to the high ground of the Missouri valley. They became known as the Hidatsa and Mandan. The figures above the map show the feathered headdresses that many Native Americans wore.

This drink bottle (above) is shaped like a mother feeding her baby. It was made at Cahokia, Illinois.

woodland

woodland and prairie

long grass prairie

short grass prairie

scrub and steppe

Writing Rock

Missouri

High Hidatsa

Low Hidatsa

Menoken

Molander

Double Ditch

Huff

Medicine Rock

Standing Rock

L. Superior

Mississippi

Thomas Riggs

Crow Creek

Sherman Park

Missouri

Medicine Creek

Pawnee Village

Fanning

Kansas

4 ADENA, HOPEWELL AND MISSISSIPPI CULTURES

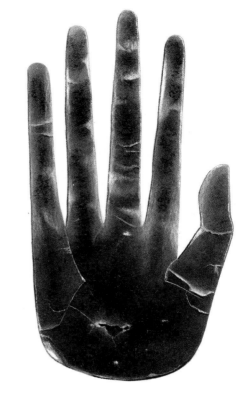

This hand (left) is made from mica, and was found in a Hopewell burial mound.

From the Great Lakes in the north to the Mississippi river delta in the south is a vast region of lakes, river valleys and wide prairies. Various cultures developed in this vast space, sharing many features – such as the building of great mounds.

First farmers and metalworkers

Many of the large animals that roamed this region in pre-historic times had died out, and hunters were forced to find new prey, or to adapt to a new way of life. Some people began to gather plants, and perhaps to plant crops them-selves. They were certainly the first Americans to work metals, from about 4000 BC. They collected surface out-crop copper and beat the rough nuggets into shape. They were able to make spears, knives, axes and fish-hooks in this way.

In the second half of the 3rd millennium BC, people began to make pottery. This skill was probably learned from more advanced neighbours to the south, in Mexico. Peoples from the south also taught the value of plants new to the settlers and perhaps the knowledge of how to plant seeds and harvest crops, such as sweetcorn (maize), beans, sunflowers and squash.

The Adena mound-builders

An important settlement was the site at Poverty Point, Louisiana, which arose about 1300 BC. Here there is a huge earth-mound, or tumulus, in the shape of a bird. Around it were other earthworks that may have shielded living areas. The size of this construction, and others like it, shows that the people who lived here were organized into a complex society, though little is known about it.

From about 1000 BC, tomb-burial became an important feature. The dead were buried in wooden tombs covered by mounds of earth, some of which (like Grave Creek Mound in West Virginia) were 20 metres (65 ft) high. The mounds often had embankments around them encircling the sacred ground and these were sometimes 100 metres (328 ft) across. About 200 mounds are known, dotted over a con-siderable area, but the central mound from which the rest radiate has been identified as the Adena Mound Group,

This scene (shown in colour on pages 16/17) shows bison hunters on the prairie. Note that the hunters have no horses (horses were extinct in America until reintroduced by the Spanish in the 1500s). The boundless prairies were home to huge wandering herds of American bison (later called buffalo by Europeans). The seasonal migration of these animals was announced by scouts and runners hastening into camp with the news. The whole tribe then made ready to hunt, and to process the animals killed.

The hunters are hiding downwind of the herd, so that their scent does not alert the animals. The shaman, wearing a wolf skin, is there to advise on the best hunting strategy. He and the hunters have already prepared for the hunt in a special ceremony.

The hunters will kill the bison with spears and bows. With skill and luck, the hunt will secure enough meat, sinews, horn and hides to sustain the tribe until next season. The bison herd goes on its way, in still countless numbers.

a large tumulus complex on the Adena estate in the Ohio valley. From this the culture gets its modern name.

The Hopewells

Pinpointing where tribes lived is difficult. As populations grew larger, people tended to stay longer in one place or even to settle permanently. As they began to farm, albeit on a primitive level, they needed permanent homes and a new social structure. Farming was still just a sideline, with most food supplied by the hunters and fishers. The Adenas also grew tobacco, which they smoked in pipes, perhaps to help induce trance states during shamans' rituals. Many pipes have been found at settlement sites.

The tradition of mound-building was followed by peoples who came after the Adena. Known as Hopewell, after the Cloud Hopewell estate in Ohio where over 30 mounds were discovered, these people were skilful craftworkers. Many fine objects have been found in burial mounds, apparently put with the body to accompany the dead person into the next world. There are jewels, clothes decorated with freshwater pearls, carved pipes, statuettes, and various kinds of ornaments. Despite lasting only 500 years or so, from about 300 BC to AD 200, Hopewell culture was rich enough to merit the title of a 'golden age'.

Hopewell trading

The Hopewell traded their goods for unusual decorative items: obsidian and bear teeth from the Rocky Mountains, shells from the Atlantic coast, mica from the Appalachians, copper and possibly gold from the Great Lakes and the Upper Mississippi valley, turtle shells, barracuda and alligator teeth from Florida and the Gulf of Mexico.

Fortunate in having a network of rivers to travel along, the Hopewell were able to trade widely, and expand into new territory. Theirs was not one single culture, but a shared system based on exchange of goods and influences between various tribes, each of which had its own organization and language, but was part of a larger cultural fabric.

For unknown reasons, this settled society collapsed suddenly. There may have been natural disasters, or wars with other Native American groups invading their territory. Whatever the cause, trade and mound-building came to a halt.

The Mississippians

Hopewell influence flowed on from the Ohio to the Mississippi, the setting for another rich culture. Here the soil was nourished by the mighty river's mud, and the waters of other rivers such as the Tennessee, Arkansas and Red. The people who lived here grew crops and even built cities, such as Cahokia (in modern Illinois). The original inhabitants of the plains were small groups of bison (buffalo) hunters. Now a more advanced culture was spread, based on crop-growing and a more settled way of life.

The Mississippians also built great earth mounds. Some were burial places. Others were temples. This culture flourished until the 1500s, when the first Europeans arrived.

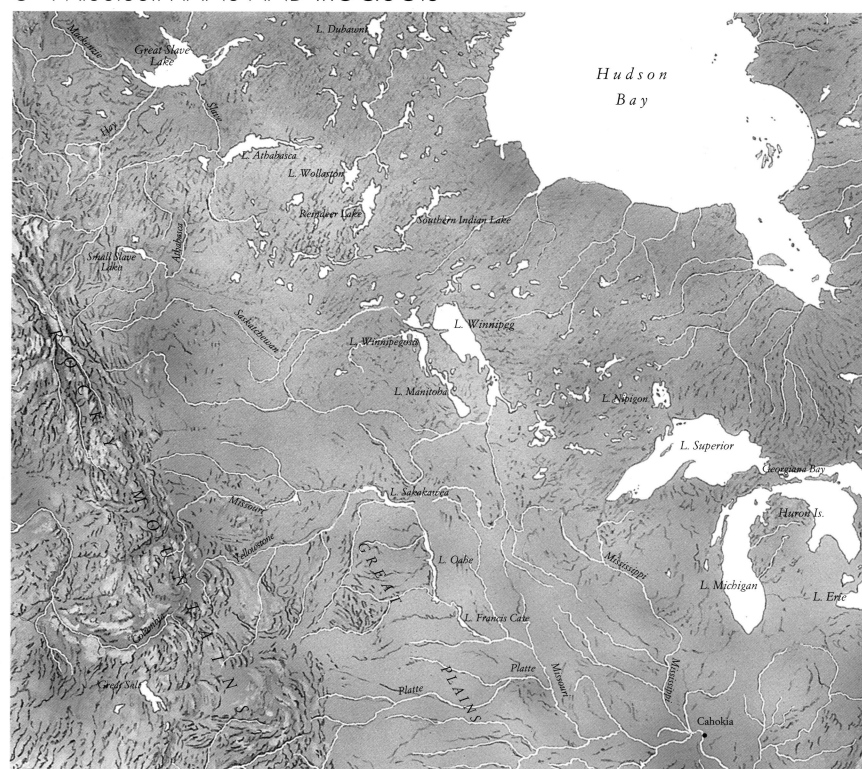

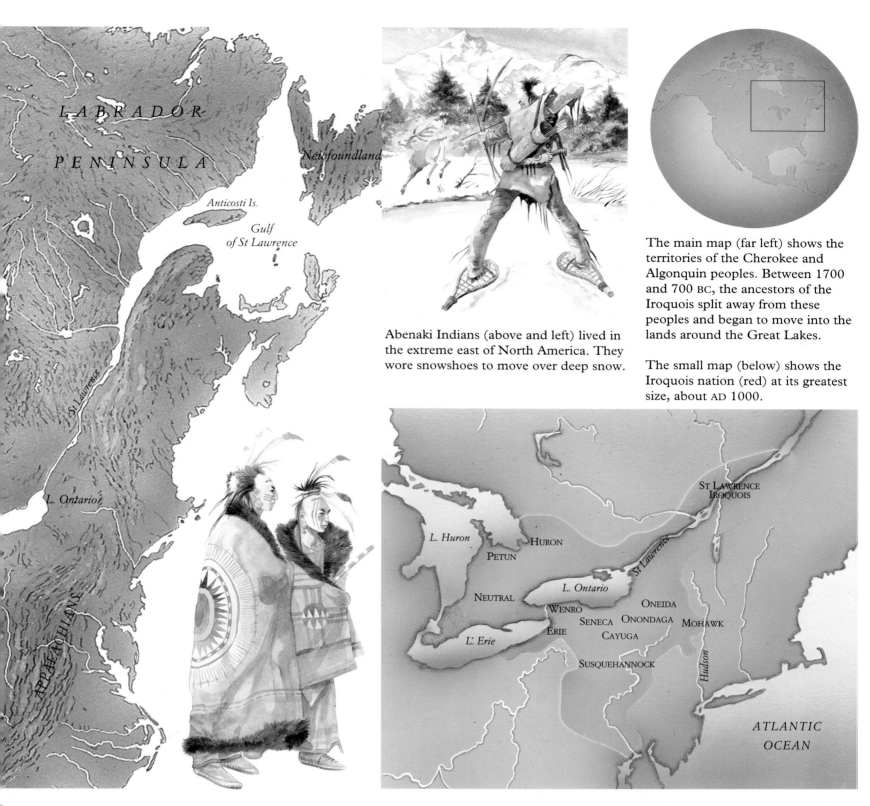

L A B R A D O R

P E N I N S U L A

Newfoundland

Anticosti Is.

Gulf of St Lawrence

St Lawrence

L. Ontario

APPALACHIANS

Abenaki Indians (above and left) lived in the extreme east of North America. They wore snowshoes to move over deep snow.

The main map (far left) shows the territories of the Cherokee and Algonquin peoples. Between 1700 and 700 BC, the ancestors of the Iroquois split away from these peoples and began to move into the lands around the Great Lakes.

The small map (below) shows the Iroquois nation (red) at its greatest size, about AD 1000.

L. Huron

PETUN

HURON

NEUTRAL

WENRO

L. Ontario

St Lawrence

ST LAWRENCE IROQUOIS

ONEIDA

SENECA ONONDAGA MOHAWK

ERIE CAYUGA

L. Erie

Hudson

SUSQUEHANNOCK

ATLANTIC OCEAN

5 MISSISSIPPIANS AND IROQUOIS

The Mississippians were able to develop an efficient and intensive method of farming, based on growing sweetcorn (maize), beans and squash. This farming economy provided the basis for a well-organized social order, with new religious beliefs and new cult practices.

There were huge new fortified centres, made from earth mound complexes, with temples on top. These settlements were sometimes very large. The biggest, Cahokia, had over a hundred mounds covering an area of almost 12 square kilometres (5 square miles). This city was founded about 600 BC and reached its maximum size about AD 1200, when some 10,000 people lived there. Soil to build the city was dug out from pits, which then filled with water to form artificial lakes. Fish from these lakes provided the people with an extra food source.

Religious ceremonies

The city government was controlled by a small group of officials and priests, who controlled food resources as well as religious activities. Ceremonies took place on top of the temple mounds, where cult objects have been found. Recurring motifs of the sun ray, the eye in the palm of the hand and the weeping eye seem to be symbols of an important Southern Cult, but little else is known about it.

The Iroquois

Bordering the lands of the Mississippians, in the dense forests of eastern North America, lived the ancestors of another powerful Native American group: the Iroquois. Their homeland was around lakes Ontario, Huron and Erie, and along the St Lawrence river.

People here lived by farming, hunting, fishing and food gathering, and this way of life lasted until the 9th century AD, about the time that the Mississippian culture began to develop. From the Mississippians, the peoples of the eastern forests learned about southern farming skills. Where the climate allowed, the Iroquois were able to grow typical Central American crops – corn, beans and squash. They also ate wild rice. They did not farm intensively, however. When the soil ceased to be fruitful, they abandoned their plots and cleared new land from the forest.

Village life in the woods

People lived in clans, a number of families sharing sections within one large house. Women played an important part

The scene below (pictured in colour on pages 20/21) shows Iroquois warriors in the woods. These people were expert at stalking forest and lake animals, such as moose, deer and beaver. They were also at home on the water, in canoes.

The men shown here are carrying stone clubs and axes. They could well be a war party. The Iroquois were brave fighters, and fought off any intruders who threatened their control over the Great Lakes and the St Lawrence river and its tributaries.

Shaving the head was a common practice among Eastern Woodland men. These warriors are wearing clothes made from furs and deerskin. They have painted faces. Some are wearing chest ornaments of porcupine quills (which also helped deflect a

blow or stone from an enemy).

The Iroquois were always on the move. Every twenty years or so, they moved their homes to a new clearing in the forest, where the soil was fresh and fertile.

This side-view picture of a man (left) is made from embossed copper plate. It comes from Craig Mound, Spiro, Oklahoma. The weeping or forked eye is a characteristic art motif of the Southern Cult.

The city of Cahokia (right) was southeast of St Louis, and was the largest pre-Columbian town in North America, north of Mexico. Its largest feature was Monk's Mound, a tumulus 300 metres (984 ft) long and more than 30 metres (98 ft) tall. There were 16 other smaller mounds, and all were enclosed on three sides by a palisade and on the fourth by the river. Outside the enclosure were dwellings and a further 100 mounds.

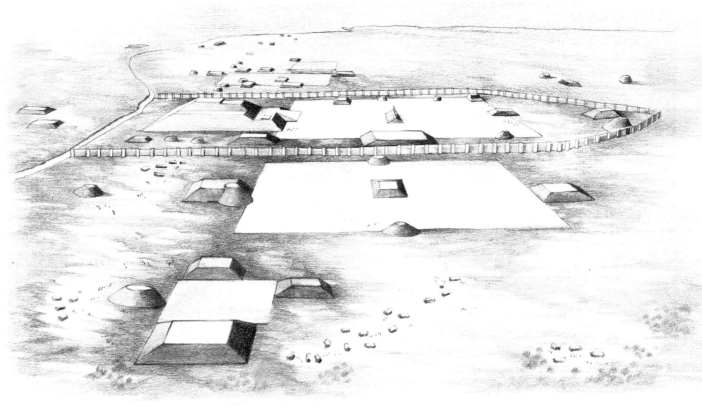

in farming, and assumed a considerable authority in decision-making within the clan.

The Iroquois were the most well organized of North American peoples. They built their houses side by side, to form orderly villages. To guard against raids from the Mississippians, they enclosed the villages with tall wooden palisades. The Iroquois formed themselves into nations. When the Europeans first contacted these people in the 1500s, they found around 12 nations, each with its own territory. Soon the number was reduced to five: Mohawk, Oneida, Cayuga, Onondaga and Seneca. In the 1600s the five formed the Iroquois League.

The reconstruction (below) shows an Iroquois village. Families shared communal long houses. The village was protected by a wooden fence or palisade.

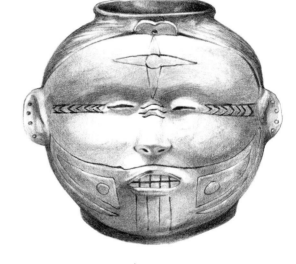

This vase (left) has a human face, with closed eyes and grimacing mouth. It is a Mississippian trophy object (representing an enemy slain in battle), and comes from near Paducah in Kentucky.

This canoe paddler (left) is wearing cult ornaments. He appears on a carved fragment of shell, and was made by the Mississippians.

These symbols (left) were important to the peoples of the Southern Cult who built the mound-temples. They are the masked and feathered eagle-dancer and (below) the plumed serpent.

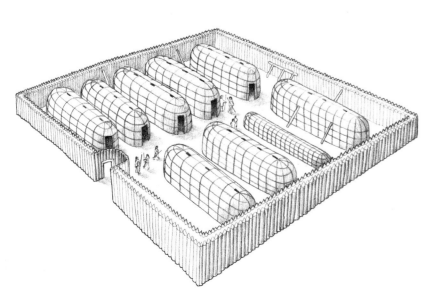

Fremont

Anasazi

Hohokam

Mogollon

Patayan

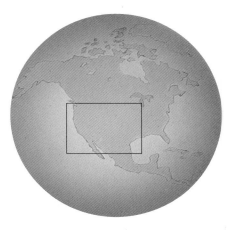

The figures in relief (left) come from Mulegé in Baja California. The main figure is coloured half in black, half in red. The others are yellow.

The main map (opposite page) shows the chief settlement sites and cultures of the Southwest. The largest groups were the Anasazi, Mogollon and Hohokam. At times one cultural area spread across another, either because some tribes shared in more than one culture, or because in a particular territory the gradual decline of one culture corresponded with the rise of another.

This is how Pueblo Bonito looked (below). People climbed ladders to get inside their homes. The innermost rooms and cellars were probably storerooms. By climbing steps, the inhabitants could reach the roof-terraces.

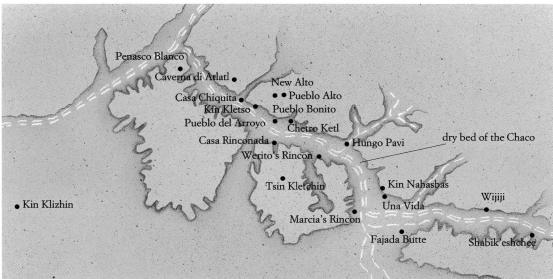

Penasco Blanco

Caverna di Atlatl

New Alto

Casa Chiquita

Pueblo Alto

Kin Kletso

Pueblo Bonito

Pueblo del Arroyo

Chetro Ketl

Casa Rinconada

Hungo Pavi

dry bed of the Chaco

Werito's Rincon

Tsin Kletchin

Kin Nahasbas

Wijiji

Una Vida

Kin Klizhin

Marcia's Rincon

Fajada Butte

Shabik'eshchee

A map of Chaco Canyon (above). This site in a remote area of New Mexico was a major centre of Anasazi culture.

6 First Farmers of the Southwest

Around 7000 BC there were great climatic changes in the American Southwest which made the region less suitable for people to live in. Once-fertile land became semi-desert as the climate became drier. The Archaic, or Desert, peoples adapted to these conditions. They gathered wild plants and hunted small animals. They were also skilful weavers and basket-makers. In time they became farmers, driven by the constant need to produce more food.

Of the later farming cultures, the three main ones were those of the Hohokam, Anasazi and Mogollon. These peoples lived in what are now the states of Arizona, New Mexico, Colorado and Utah.

The Hohokam

The name Hohokam means 'Disappeared' or 'Dead'. These people lived in southern Arizona, between the Gila and Snake rivers. When they lived is less certain, but it was between 600 and 300 BC. They may have come from Central America, or simply had close links with Mexican cultures because there was regular trade between them. Either way, there is much to show that the culture of Mexico was a strong influence on Hohokam buildings and arts, and on their farming methods.

The land was very dry, so the Hohokam had to build irrigation systems to water it. They were the first people in North America to undertake complex irrigation schemes by building impressive dams, changing the courses of rivers, and digging a network of canals many kilometres in length. This was very hard work, but it made possible the harvesting of two crops a year.

The most important Hohokam settlement was Snaketown, near Phoenix, Arizona. It was founded about 300 BC and people lived there for some 1,500 years. The presence among the Hohokam of large ceremonial centres, quite different from those in villages, suggests that towns were the focal points for whole communities. Indeed it is likely that the Hohokam had a centralized organization, with the town temples at its heart.

The mounds on which the temples stood were low pyramid shapes, like those of Central America. There were also ball-game courts, similar to those of the Central American peoples. Houses were built by digging pits, and roofing the pits with reed mats spread with mud and clay. Decorated and engraved shells are among the distinctive objects found at Hohokam sites.

The Anasazi

The name Anasazi means 'Old Ones' in the Navajo language. These people appeared on the scene about AD 200, as hunters and food-gatherers. They were expert weavers, and were called Basket Makers. Later, they began to make pottery and to farm.

Between AD 500 and 700, the Anasazi mastered the skills needed to grow the 'classic' American crops: corn, beans and squash. They gave up their pit-dwellings and built

The scene (shown in colour on pages 24/25) is of Anasazi people in their pueblo near Mesa Verde, southern Colorado. The houses are sturdy, stone-built structures, with flat roofs supported by timbers. People climb stone steps and wooden ladders to reach the upper levels.

Inside the buildings, they climb ladders lowered through holes in the ceilings to reach the upper rooms. The kivas, or ceremonial chambers, are underground.

The houses are set against the rock wall of the canyon, for protection and to make building easier. Rock paintings can be seen on the cliff face.

The woman on the left is weaving a reed basket. Weaving was one of the Anasazi's many skills. They made baskets, mats, figures for religious use, and even water containers woven from reeds. Much of this work was done by women, who were also the community farmers. The men did the hunting. The Anasazi also made pottery, as can be seen here. Two painted bowls are on the left and the men in the centre of the picture are shaping other pots from wet clay.

The two animals (opposite page) are made from reeds, and come from the Grand Canyon. They date from the Archaic period.

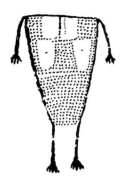

These rock carvings (left and right) came from Grand Gulch Canyon in southeastern Utah. The people are known as Basket Makers, and the patterns in the carvings show their clothing.

These rock carvings (below), in the style known as Fremont, were found at Fruita Point, Capitol Reef, in southern Utah.

The jug (below) is in a geometric style. It was found at Mesa Verde in Colorado and dates from the 11th century.

houses with from one to three floors, using rows of square-trimmed stones for the walls. The Spanish explorers who first saw the Anasazi villages called them 'pueblo', meaning 'town', and the name has stuck; it is still used for the descendants of the Anasazi.

The villagers used ladders to climb up to the top floors of their houses. They held many religious ceremonies, and a special underground chamber, the kiva, was kept for such ceremonies and meetings. Religion was very important; the chiefs were religious leaders, believed to be guided by the spirits.

In the desert, villages were built close to rocky outcrops, for protection from the weather and from enemy attack. Some were built in steep-walled rock canyons. The largest of the Anasazi settlements, known as Pueblo Bonito, is in Chaco Canyon. It is a complex with more than 800 rooms, on four floors, built between 950 and 1130 at a time when Anasazi culture was flourishing.

Although they shared many common traditions, the Anasazi were split into various groups, and there were at least six different languages among them. Their influence reached surrounding areas, particularly the mountains between Arizona and New Mexico. This was the home of the Mogollon, or Mountain People.

The Mogollon

Mogollon culture arose in the AD 300s, when it was still based mainly on hunting and gathering. In the years that followed, the Mogollon perfected their farming skills, beginning to specialize in crops such as wheat, beans, squash, tobacco and cotton. They were fortunate in having reasonable environmental and climatic conditions, especially near to the rivers. Like the Anasazi, the Mogollon changed from living in pit-dwellings to pueblo-style apartment blocks. The ceremonial kiva was now the only part of the structure that was underground.

Mogollon culture vanished between the 1100s and 1300s, perhaps as the result of being absorbed by the Anasazi. The Hohokam disappeared at much the same time. Other causes of these disappearances may have been climate change, natural disasters, or violent raids by new foes, the Apaches. Whatever the reason, these ingenious farming peoples vanished. The Anasazi, too, went into decline, even before the arrival of Europeans in the 1500s.

This fragment of a pottery vase (below) is one of the few Anasazi art-objects to show a realistic human face. It is from Pueblo Bonito, New Mexico, and was made about 1100.

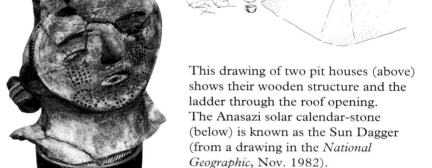

This drawing of two pit houses (above) shows their wooden structure and the ladder through the roof opening. The Anasazi solar calendar-stone (below) is known as the Sun Dagger (from a drawing in the *National Geographic*, Nov. 1982).

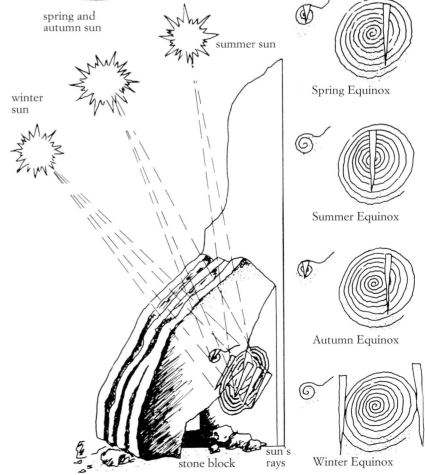

spring and autumn sun

summer sun

winter sun

Spring Equinox

Summer Equinox

Autumn Equinox

stone block   sun's rays   Winter Equinox

7 FARMERS AND VILLAGERS OF MESOAMERICA

The main map (right) shows Archaic and Formative period sites in Mesoamerica. The continuous occupation of these lands despite their increasing aridity shows the adaptability of the peoples.

The small map (below) shows the four main language areas of Mesoamerica. At one time more than 200 languages were spoken, which scholars have grouped into 22 families, 19 of which belong to the four groups. Some languages are dead, but many are still in use.

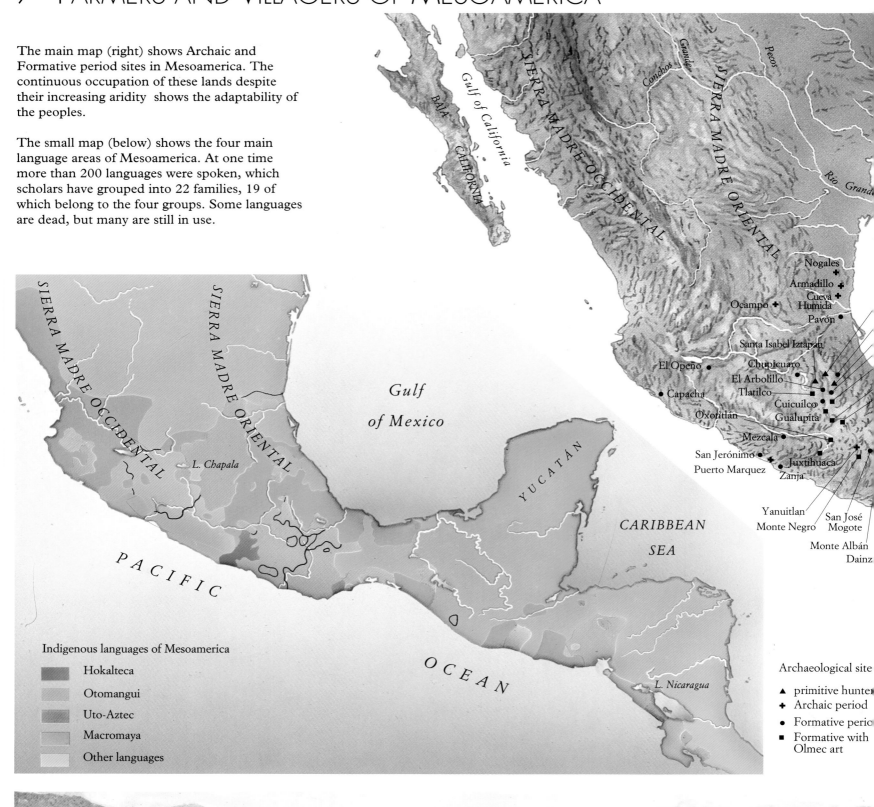

Indigenous languages of Mesoamerica

- Hokalteca
- Otomangui
- Uto-Aztec
- Macromaya
- Other languages

Archaeological site

- ▲ primitive hunter
- ✚ Archaic period
- ● Formative period
- ■ Formative with Olmec art

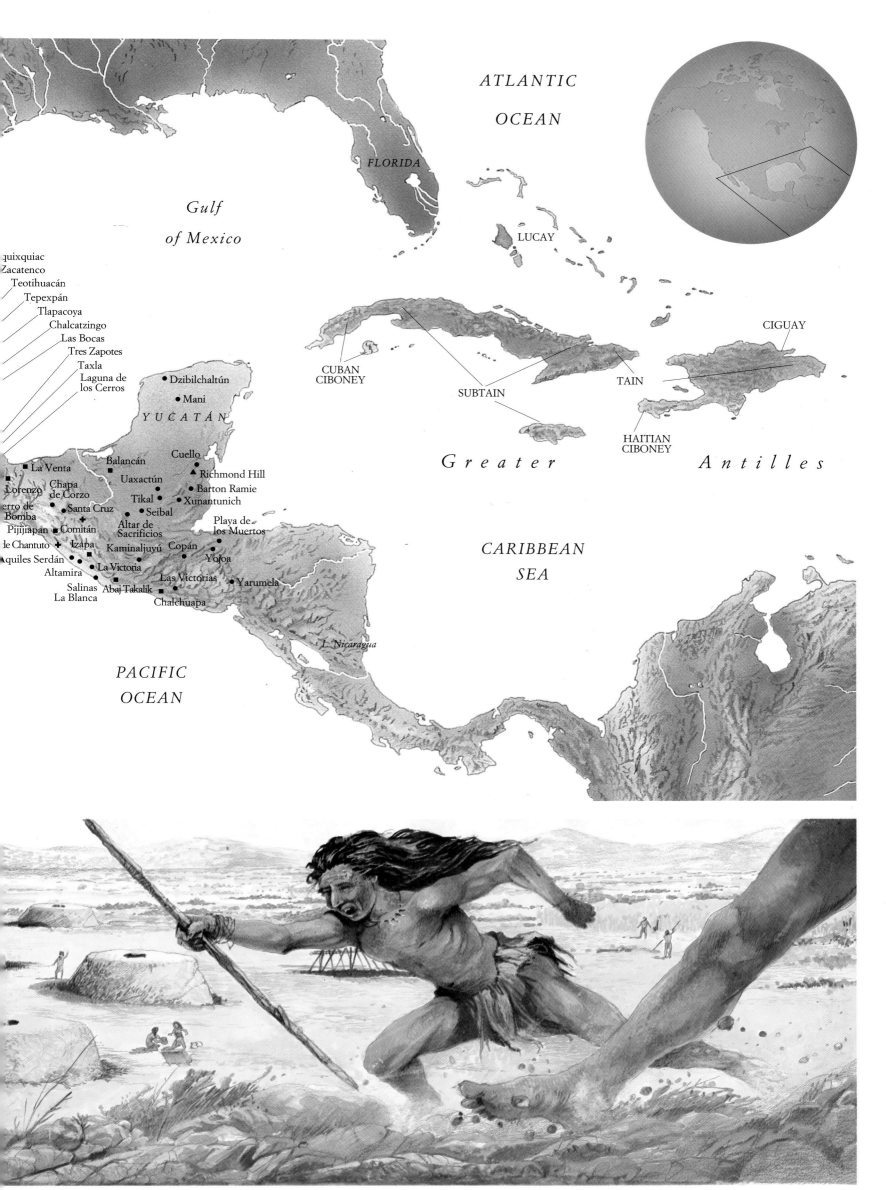

ATLANTIC

OCEAN

FLORIDA

Gulf

of Mexico

LUCAY

CIGUAY

quixquiac
Zacatenco
Teotihuacán
Tepexpán
Tlapacoya
Chalcatzingo
Las Bocas
Tres Zapotes
Taxla
Laguna de
los Cerros

• Dzibilchaltún

• Mani

Y U C A T Á N

CUBAN
CIBONEY

SUBTAIN

TAIN

HAITIAN
CIBONEY

• Cuello

Balancán

Uaxactún

▲ Richmond Hill

• Barton Ramie

Tikal • Xunantunich

■ La Venta

Chapa
de Corzo

Lorenzo

erro de
Bomba

Pijijiapan ■ Comitán

le Chantuto ✛ Izapa

aquiles Serdán

Altamira

Salinas
La Blanca

• Santa Cruz

• Seibal

Altar de
Sacrificios

La Victoria

Abaj Takalik

Kaminaljuyú

Las Victorias

Chalchuapa

Copán

• Yojoa

Playa de
los Muertos

• Yarumela

G r e a t e r

A n t i l l e s

CARIBBEAN

SEA

L. Nicaragua

PACIFIC

OCEAN

As the glaciers retreated at the end of the last Ice Age, the hills and mountains of Mesoamerica, or 'Middle America', changed dramatically. In this area (modern Mexico and Central America), what had once been vast prairies became deserts, as temperatures rose and rainfall fell. Herds of mammoth and mastodon no longer roamed the grasslands. People relied more and more on gathering wild plants. From about 7000 BC they began to plant crops. This period is known as the Archaic or Early Farming period and, according to some experts, coincided with the development of agriculture in the Old World (Europe, Africa and Asia).

From evidence found in caves and rock shelters (dry overhangs under cliffs), such as those in the Tehuacán valley in Puebla (Mexico), it seems that small bands of people began to grow wild plants, including corn, squash, beans and peppers. Some plants such as gourds could be used as water containers or as floats for fishing nets.

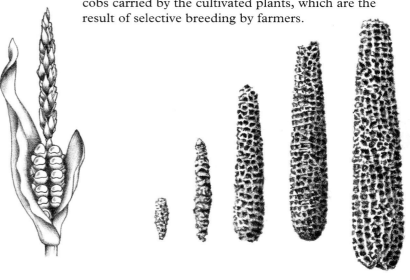

These dried corn cobs (below), probably from wild maize plants, were found in the San Marcos Cave in the Tehuacán valley, Mexico. The native wild corn produced a tiny cob, compared with the much larger cobs carried by the cultivated plants, which are the result of selective breeding by farmers.

The first farmers

Between 7000 and 5000 BC, people began living in camps and cave-settlements for seasons at a time. They were semi-nomads, gathering seeds and waiting for vegetables to ripen for picking before moving on. They probably planted a few small plots with avocados, chilies and squash.

By about 5000 BC, a primitive type of domesticated corn was being grown. Where this corn came from, and how it was developed as a crop plant, is not clear. It was obviously a useful food source, for pestles and grindstones were made to pound the kernels into flour.

People no longer depended on hunting wild animals for food, though hunting still went on. By 3000 BC people in Mesoamerica were using stone pots and beakers. This evidence shows that they were staying in one place, for such items would be heavy to carry around. Between 2200 and 1500 BC, pottery was being made, a sure sign that the nomads had become settled dwellers.

Village life and new skills

Besides those in the Tehuacán valley, early farming settlements have been found in Oaxaca, and along the coasts of the Gulf of Mexico in Veracruz. In northern Belize, people grew manioc, just as the hill people grew corn. Living near to the sea, these people were also able to collect shellfish and catch fish from the ocean and from river estuaries.

Plant domestication and settlement went together, and

The scene below (pictured in colour on pages 28/29) shows a village in Archaic Mexico. The people have settled near a river, which provides precious drinking water and supports wild plants, which they gather to eat. They can also catch fish in the river, using dugout canoes. Women make nets and weave fish traps.

The houses are pit-dwellings, made by digging a hole which is then roofed over with a framework of sticks plastered with clay and straw. Smoke from the fire drifts out through a hole in the roof.

To the left is a crude open kiln, for hardening pottery made of clay that the people dig out from a nearby claypit. In the background, on the right, is a cornfield.

Despite this new food source, men still hunt armadillos and other animals, as their ancestors did. They also catch hares, lizards and birds. The prey is hung on poles for skinning, and some meat will be dried to preserve it.

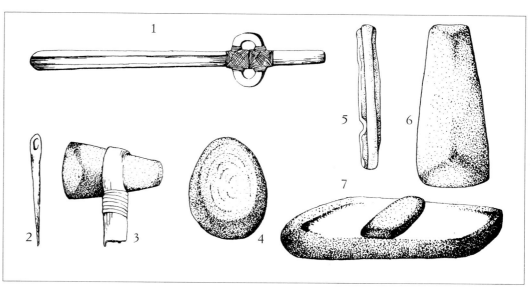

This is the face (below) of an Archaic hunter-gatherer from Mexico, as reconstructed by a modern artist.

These utensils (right) were found at Cuicuilco in Mexico, and date from between 7,000 and 4,000 years ago.
1. spear-thrower made of deer antler
2. bone needle
3. stone axe bound to wooden handle
4. stone hammer
5. obsidian blade
6. stone chisel
7. stone grindstone and grinder for grinding corn

This is an example (below) of an early Mexican temple building, set on a stone base with steps and terraces. The drawing is based on a find in the Tlapacoya Valley, dating from about 400 BC.

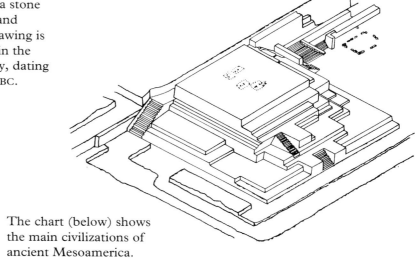

The chart (below) shows the main civilizations of ancient Mesoamerica.

the first farmers began to develop better plants, by selecting those wild varieties that grew best and gave the best yields. This meant more food, and a growing population. The Archaic culture gave way to a more advanced way of life, known to scholars as the Formative, or Pre-Classical, period. This was a time when the first villages were built, and people made much better utensils, including dishes made from smooth-rubbed stone for food preparation, pottery, rush baskets, ropes from plant fibres, and clay figurines which heralded the beginnings of sculpture.

This change took place in Mexico between about 2000 and 1600 BC, and may have occurred at about the same time in the hotter coastal regions of the Pacific coast, from Chiapas to Guatemala.

The growth of the village

Throughout Mesoamerica, people began to live in villages of thatched houses. Everywhere they made clay statues and pots, and wove cotton. There were three main phases of the Formative Period in Mesoamerica: the Lower (2000 to 900 BC), Middle (900 to 300 BC) and Upper (300 BC to the early centuries AD). During these phases, simple village communities lived alongside more developed societies, ruled by kings or priests.

The five regions

Five archaeological regions are associated with the Formative period. One is that of the Maya, which extends through part of Honduras, Belize, Guatemala and south-eastern Mexico. Another extends across Oaxaca state (Mexico) and is represented by the Mixtec and Zapotec civilizations. There is a Gulf Coast region, where the Olmecs and Totonacs lived, and in the heart of Mexico, the Central Plateau region, where the Teotihuacán, Toltecs and Aztecs were the most powerful influences. Western Mexico developed its own regional cultures, which later enveloped the rest of Mesoamerica.

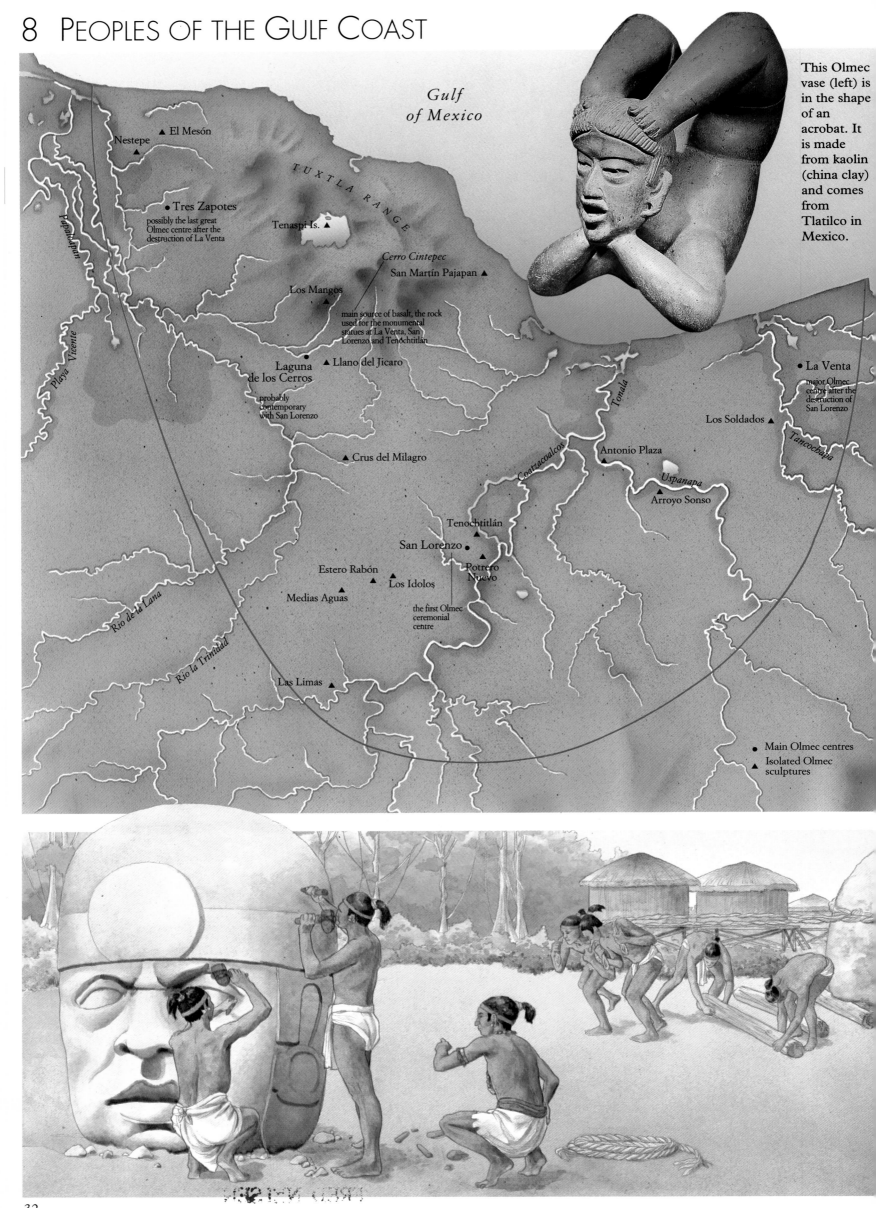

Gulf of Mexico

Nestepe ▲

▲ El Mesón

• Tres Zapotes
possibly the last great
Olmec centre after the
destruction of La Venta

TUXTLA RANGE

Tenaspi Is. ▲

Cerro Cintepec

San Martín Pajapan ▲

Los Mangos

main source of basalt, the rock
used for the monumental
statues at La Venta, San
Lorenzo and Tenochtitlán

Papaloapan

Playa Vicente

Laguna
de los Cerros

probably
contemporary
with San Lorenzo

▲ Llano del Jicaro

Tonala

• La Venta
major Olmec
centre after the
destruction of
San Lorenzo

Los Soldados ▲

Tancochapa

▲ Crus del Milagro

Coatzacoalcos

Antonio Plaza •

Uspanapa

Arroyo Sonso ▲

Tenochtitlán ▲

San Lorenzo •

Estero Rabón ▲

▲ Los Idolos

Potrero
Nuevo ▲

the first Olmec
ceremonial
centre

Rio de la Lana

Medias Aguas ▲

Rio la Trinidad

Las Limas ▲

• Main Olmec centres
▲ Isolated Olmec
sculptures

This Olmec
vase (left) is
in the shape
of an
acrobat. It
is made
from kaolin
(china clay)
and comes
from
Tlatilco in
Mexico.

This group of small votive figures (left), made of jade and serpentine, stands in a semicircle of symbolic axe-stones at La Venta, Tabasco, Mexico.

This huge head (below) is known as Monument 17. It is one of eight colossal heads found at San Lorenzo, and shows an Olmec ruler. The head was carved in basalt from the Tuxtla Mountains.

The main map (left) shows the original area of Olmec influence. The smaller map (below) shows where the Olmecs sought the minerals they needed, and which their own territory lacked.

Gulf
of Mexico

Tlatilco
Tlapacoya
El Vejión
Gualupita
Las Bocas
Chalcatzingo
Tres Zapotes
La Venta
Oxotitlan Cave
Laguna de
los Cerros
Juxtlahuaca
Cave
San Lorenzo

Mineral deposits

▲ Basalt, used for Olmec monuments

■ Obsidian, for San Lorenzo

□ Iron, used for mirrors

+ Serpentine, for carvings

● Olmec site/ Olmec influence

PACIFIC
OCEAN

8 PEOPLES OF THE GULF COAST

The Olmec people built the first sophisticated civilization of Mesoamerica, which influenced later cultures of the region. It sprang from a group of Neolithic farmers, with perhaps some influences from Ecuador and Colombia in South America.

Where the Olmecs lived

Much of what we know of the Olmecs comes from recent studies of their sites. Their civilization began about 1700 BC and reached a peak between 1200 and 300 BC. Thereafter it declined, until by AD 200 it had ended. Olmec culture can be seen in the Mexican states of southern Veracruz and western Tabasco, the wettest region of the Gulf coast. It seems also to have spread to other regions, including Puebla, Oaxaca, Chiapas and what is now Guatemala. The Olmecs had enormous influence over other peoples who, from about 1000 BC, settled between the Gulf coast and the foothills of the Sierra Madre Occidental mountains. These cultures are known as Veracruz Centre Cultures.

One of the ways in which the Olmecs exerted influence on neighbours was through trade. They were eager to obtain raw materials, especially semi-precious stones such as amethyst, turquoise, black serpentine and jade.

How they lived

The early Olmecs lived in straw huts, built on top of earth mounds. Their villages were made up of family groups of relatives, led by a shaman or by a council of elders. They lived by farming, growing corn, chilies, beans and squash. They gathered wild plants, collected shellfish from the

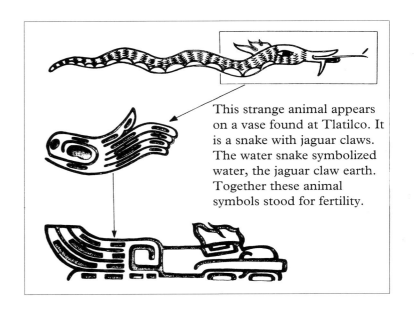

This strange animal appears on a vase found at Tlatilco. It is a snake with jaguar claws. The water snake symbolized water, the jaguar claw earth. Together these animal symbols stood for fertility.

shores and swamps, and hunted wild animals, with spear-throwers made from deer antlers, and with nets.

The Olmecs made pottery, mainly single-colour bowls and plates, painted jars, figurines of men and women, and musical instruments. They wove cloth from plant fibres, and made objects from bone and semi-precious stones. Their religion was based on a totem cult, in which the jaguar and snake were prominent, linked to the fertility of the soil, life-giving water and the importance of crops.

Between 1200 and 900 BC some Gulf coast villages grew into much bigger settlements, and served as ceremonial centres for the surrounding region. The main centres were La Venta, San Lorenzo, Tres Zapotes, Cerro de las Mesas and Las Limas. They had large, man-made mounds or platforms, sited on a north-south line. These mounds were made from earth, faced with unfired bricks and coloured clay. On the mounds, altars and stelae (ritual stones) were set up. Administrative buildings and temples also stood on

This scene (in colour on pages 32/33) shows Olmec artists at work making head-sculptures. The heavy blocks of stone used to make these curious monuments had to be floated on rafts along rivers or dragged overland on wooden rollers. Here, workers toil to drag an uncut block on to the work site, while sculptors put the finishing touches to a head that has been given the characteristic flattened features. They are using stone chisels and hammers.

In the background is the village. The Olmecs usually lived close to water, near lagoons or marshes. Some villages grew into larger towns, the first in Mesoamerica, and here the Olmecs erected their mound-buildings, faced with mud bricks. They also made paved streets.

The Olmecs used improved tools, such as quartz drills, serpentine scrapers, basalt mallets and wooden wedges (for splitting rocks) to aid them in these massive projects.

The purpose of the stone heads is not clear. They may have represented sacrificial victims, whose presence served to protect the village from danger.

The bird at the right is a quetzal, a creature of the forest with long tail feathers that Mesoamerican chiefs often wore as symbols of power.

This black pot (below) shows a freshwater fish. It was engraved with its decoration while the clay was still soft and comes from Tlatilco.

This basalt statue (below) from Veracruz, Mexico, is known as 'The Wrestler'.

Jaguar House (above) is an Olmec tomb made from 44 columns of basalt rock. It is at Villahermosa in Tabasco state, Mexico.

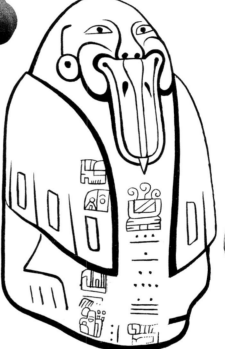

This statuette (left), made of nephrite (a mineral), shows a man wearing a duck mask. Picture-writing inscriptions on it date this object to AD 162. It comes from San Andres in Veracruz, Mexico.

This huge head (below) with round earrings is from Monte Alto in Guatemala.

the terraced mounds. The centres had marketplaces and a court where a ball game, in some ways a mixture of basketball and pelota, was played.

Trade and government

The number and variety of sculptures and ornaments fashioned from different stones make it clear that mining for minerals was an important activity. The Olmecs traded for these materials, travelling along waterways on rafts and canoes, as well as overland.

The government seems to have been highly centralized, for the size and splendour of Olmec constructions at their peak suggest a well-organized society. Power rested with the priest-nobility, who ruled over the workers and merchants. These lower orders contributed greatly to Olmec civilization, but owned little of the best farmland: this was concentrated in the hands of the ruling few.

The Olmec heads

The Olmec sculptures are distinctive. They frequently show human figures, or huge heads with thick, protruding lips, slanted eyes, and wide, flat noses. Figures are sometimes seated or standing. Totem-like human-animal figures are also found. There are carved stones, with inscriptions, tombs and ceremonial altars, as well as small pieces of fine workmanship, such as pendants, earrings, masks and axe blades. Jade, schist and granite were favourite materials.

Before 300 BC, the Olmec culture began to decline. New cultures, shaped by other peoples' contact with the Olmecs, developed and laid the foundations for the great civilizations of Classic Mesoamerica. During the period AD 300 to 600 new centres such as Las Mesas, Xiuhtetelco, Yohualinchan, Quiahuiztlan and Isla de Sacrificios were growing in importance. A new and important religious centre developed at El Tajín, in the Veracruz region, between AD 600 and 900.

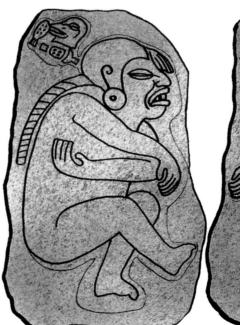

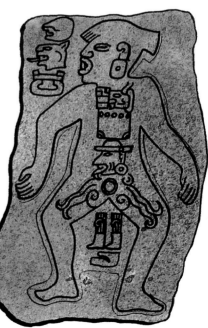

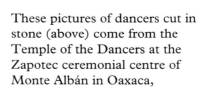

These pictures of dancers cut in stone (above) come from the Temple of the Dancers at the Zapotec ceremonial centre of Monte Albán in Oaxaca, Mexico. One of the important cultures influenced by the Olmecs was that of the Zapotecs, who are described in the next section.

9 MEXICO'S CENTRAL PLATEAU AND OAXACA

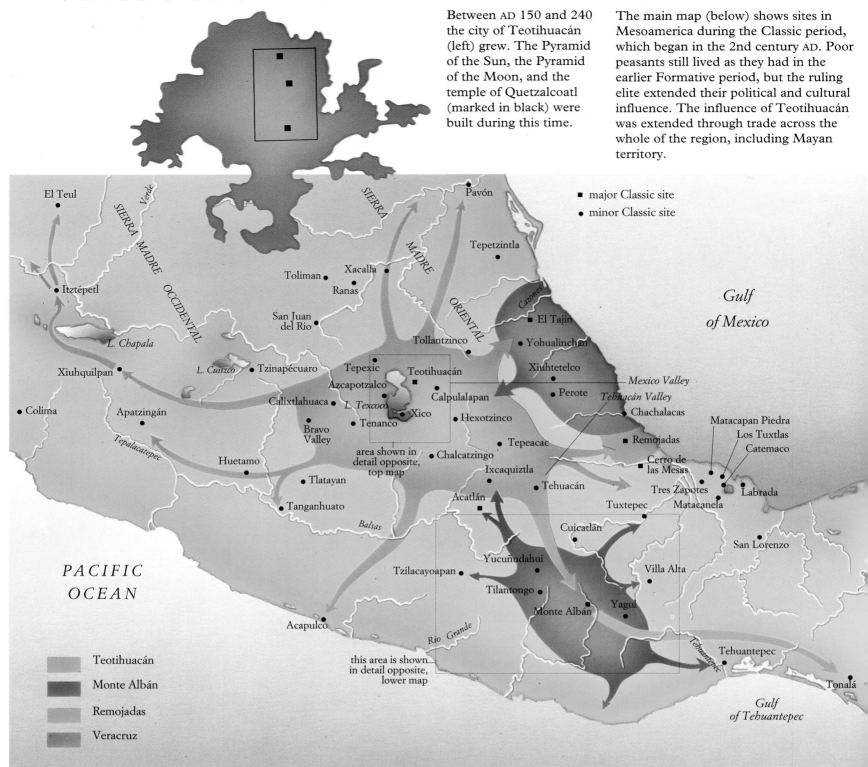

Between AD 150 and 240 the city of Teotihuacán (left) grew. The Pyramid of the Sun, the Pyramid of the Moon, and the temple of Quetzalcoatl (marked in black) were built during this time.

The main map (below) shows sites in Mesoamerica during the Classic period, which began in the 2nd century AD. Poor peasants still lived as they had in the earlier Formative period, but the ruling elite extended their political and cultural influence. The influence of Teotihuacán was extended through trade across the whole of the region, including Mayan territory.

■ major Classic site
● minor Classic site

Gulf of Mexico

El Teul
SIERRA MADRE OCCIDENTAL
Verde
Itztépetl
L. Chapala
Xiuhquilpan
Colima
L. Cuitzco
Tzinapécuaro
Apatzingán
Tepalacatepec
Huetamo
Tlatayan
Tanganhuato

Toliman
Xacalla
Ranas
San Juan del Rio
Tepexic
Azcapotzalco
Calixtlahuaca
L. Texcoco
Tenanco
Xico
Bravo Valley

SIERRA MADRE ORIENTAL
Pavón
Tepetzintla
Cazones
El Tajín
Tollantzinco
Yohualinchan
Xiuhtetelco
Teotihuacán
Calpulalapan
Perote
Mexico Valley
Tehuacán Valley
Chachalacas
Hexotzinco
Tepeacac
Remojadas
Ixcaquiztla
Chalcatzingo
Tehuacán
Cerro de las Mesas
Matacapan Piedra
Los Tuxtlas
Catemaco
Tres Zapotes
Labrada
Matacanela

area shown in detail opposite, top map

Acatlán
Balsas
Cuicatlán
Tuxtepec
San Lorenzo

PACIFIC OCEAN

Yucuñudahui
Tzilacayoapan
Tilantongo
Monte Albán
Yagul
Villa Alta

Acapulco
Rio Grande
this area is shown in detail opposite, lower map

Tehuantepec
Tonalá
Gulf of Tehuantepec

Teotihuacán
Monte Albán
Remojadas
Veracruz

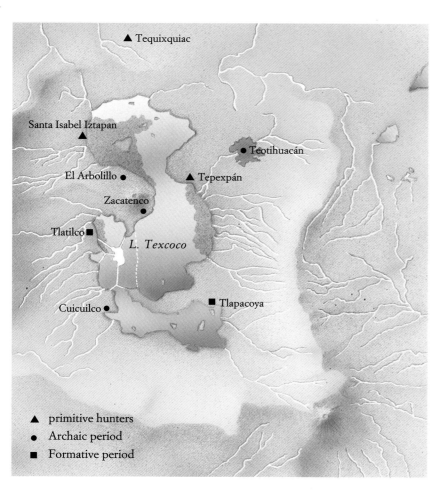

Tequixquiac

Santa Isabel Iztapan

Teotihuacán

El Arbolillo

Tepexpán

Zacatenco

Tlatilco

L. Texcoco

Cuicuilco

Tlapacoya

▲ primitive hunters
● Archaic period
■ Formative period

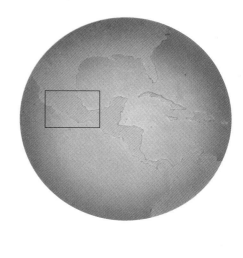

The map (left) shows important settlements around Lake Texcoco. The lake later became the heart of the Aztec civilization and now (almost drained) has been swallowed by Mexico City.

The Oaxaca valley (below left) was the centre of Zapotec (red) and Mixtec (blue) settlements. Monte Albán is a particularly important site in the region.

The timechart (below) shows the development of Zapotec and Mixtec cultures.

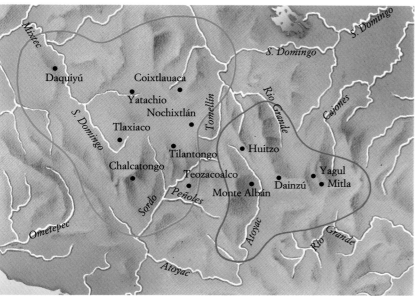

Mixtec

Daquíyú

Coixtlauaca

S. Domingo

S. Domingo

Yatachio

Nochixtlán

Tomellín

Río Grande

Cajones

Tlaxiaco

Tilantongo

Huitzo

Chalcatongo

Teozacoalco

Yagul

Peñoles

Monte Albán

Dainzú

Mitla

Ometepec

Sordo

Atoyac

Río Grande

Atoyac

period	date	ZAPOTECS		MIXTECS			
		Oaxaca Valley		period	date	Upper Mixtec	Lower Mixtec
		phase				phase	phase
POST-CLASSIC	1521	Monte Albán V		POST-CLASSIC	1521	Late Natividad	
	1325	Monte Albán IV			1100	Early Natividad	
	800	Monte Albán IIIB			800	Las Flores	
CLASSIC	650		Monte Albán IIIA	CLASSIC/ TOWNS	600	Huamelulpan III	Ñuiñe
		Monte Albán II-IIIA			300		
	250		Monte Albán II		200	Ramos Huamelulpan II	un-defined
FORMATIVE OR PRE-CLASSIC	100 BC				100 BC		
	0	Monte Albán II			0		
	100 BC				100 BC	Ramos I	Ñudée
	500	Monte Albán I			500		
	700	Rosario		PRE-CLASSIC/ VILLAGE	800	Late Cruz	
	800	Guadalupe				Middle Cruz	
	1200	San José			1200	Early Cruz	
	1500	Tierras Largas		ARCHAIC OR LITHIC	1500		
ARCHAIC OR LITHIC	3000				3700		
	5000						

9 MEXICO'S CENTRAL PLATEAU AND OAXACA

This stone skull (below) still has traces of its original red paint. It is ringed by rays, and symbolizes the star that falls to light the way for the dead into the next world. It was found in front of the Pyramid of the Sun at Teotihuacán.

As the Olmecs declined, the Mexico valley region became less important. But in Mexico's central plateau region there arose a new civilization with an influence felt throughout Mesoamerica. This was Teotihuacán, named after a valley in the northeast of the plateau. The main settlement was a city with a population estimated at more than 125,000, and covering an area of some 20 square kilometres (8 square miles).

The city was planned on a grid system, suggesting that most of it was built at the same time. The people had fertile soils south of the valley in which to grow crops. There were lakes nearby and abundant wildlife to hunt in the mountains. Present, too, were rich deposits of obsidian, and the strategic location of the city gave its inhabitants control over the trade routes with their neighbours.

Artificial islands and trade

The basis of agriculture in Teotihuacán was irrigation, which was well developed. The people built artificial islands in the lakes and river marshlands to create extra space for crops.

Teotihuacán grew strong through trade. Its people had a monopoly in the sale óf obsidian, and among them there emerged a merchant class, buying and selling across Mesoamerica. They bought in products such as cotton, cacao, avocados, jade, turquoise, and birds' feathers, which were used as personal adornments and in clothing for the wealthy.

The social order was based on families or related groups of people, who lived together in housing complexes and carried on the same trades or crafts, as labourers, builders, painters and so on. The family heads were in charge of the group's activities, and through agreements with neighbouring heads of other family-trade groups, these leaders created a ruling class of administrators. The city developed an efficient government, which controlled religion, politics, economics and the military. From the city, this government's control extended over a wide area.

Tula

In AD 750, at the end of the Classic period, Teotihuacán

The picture below (shown in colour on pages 36/37) is an artist's view of the impressive city of Teotihuacán, the 'place where gods are made'. The city site was on a plateau, surrounded by mountains and plains. It was crossed by the San Juan river.

The city has large pyramids, made from earth spread over with plaster. Stone blocks are fitted together, as can be seen in the terracing on the left of the picture. Steps lead up the sides of the pyramids to temple buildings on top. Two wide main streets cross the city. This is the Street of the Dead, leading to the Plaza, or Square of the Pyramid of the Moon. It is lined with large buildings. Among them are the Pyramid of the Sun, the huge step-pyramid on the left, the Temple of Agriculture and the Palace of Jaguars. At the southern end of the avenue is the Citadel, the centre of government. In front of this complex people bring goods to sell in the large marketplace.

The huge public buildings dominate the central area; the small dwellings of the city's people are clustered on the outskirts. There are special compounds for each trade group, such as merchants, as well as residential apartment blocks for the well-to-do, with beautiful frescoes (wall paintings) decorating the rooms.

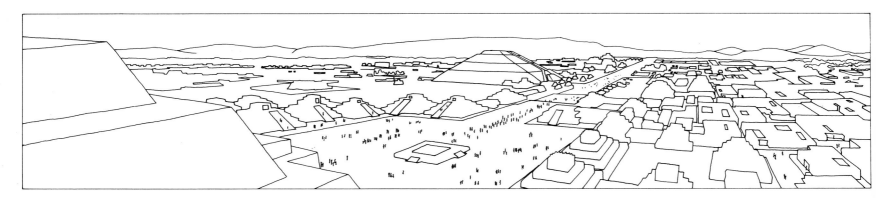

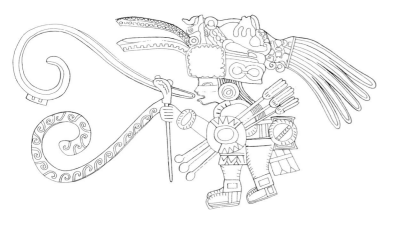

This wall painting (left) from Teotihuacán is of a warrior.

A terracotta statuette (right) from Guerrerro state, Mexico, has moving limbs and is possibly a child's toy.

This wall painting (below) shows a person, perhaps a priest, dressed as a jaguar and entering a temple. It comes from the Pyramid of the Moon at Teotihuacán.

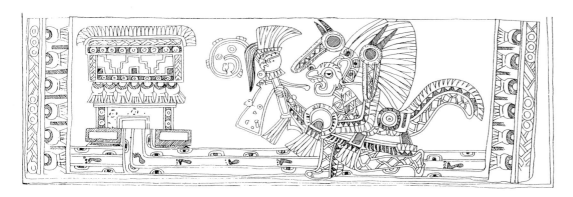

The Mixtecs used a form of picture-writing, seen on this calendar (right) of 20 named days. It was used for ritual purposes.

This carved skull-like head (below) is part of a building, and was found near the Pyramid of the Sun, Teotihuacán.

Alligator

Monkey

Wind

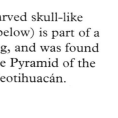
Grass

House

Cane

Lizard

Jaguar

Snake

Eagle

Death

Buzzard

Deer

Movement

Rabbit

Flint knife

Water

Rain

Dog

Flower

fell. People from the north, including the Nonoalcas and Toltec-Chichimecs, pushed into Teotihuacán territory. New cities grew up, among which were Xiochicalco, Cholula and Cacaxtla. But the most important was Tula, which became the major centre of the Toltecs in the period AD 900 to 1200. For a while, Tula was the mightiest power in Mexico.

Zapotecs of Monte Albán

In Oaxaca, other peoples were also in the ascendancy: the Zapotecs and Mixtecs. The Zapotecs were originally farmers, who had been strongly influenced by Olmec culture. By 500 BC they had begun to organize themselves into small states, each based on a village ceremonial centre to which local farmers came for religious rituals. These states formed alliances, until eventually they merged into one powerful state with its capital at Monte Albán. This is one of the most spectacular religious centres of Mesoamerica, laid out on a mountain top. Its palaces and temples were constructed over the centuries to AD 900.

The Mixtecs

Monte Albán and Teotihuacán seem to have co-existed on peaceful terms. But when Teotihuacán fell, Monte Albán also weakened. Smaller groups of people, such as the Cuilapan, Mitla, Zaachila, Yagul and others struggled among themselves. The warlike Mixtecs, a people from the mountains according to legend, gained control over the Zapotec empire. By AD 1000 the Mixtecs controlled the whole region of Oaxaca in Mexico. Although they often fought among themselves, they were united when fighting their rivals, the Aztecs.

The Mixtec pottery vase (left) is decorated with a death-figure.

A drawing (below) of the ball-game court in the Great Plaza of Monte Albán.

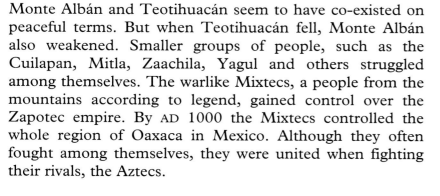

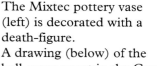

10 THE MAYA

The map (right) shows the main sites of Maya settlement during the Late Formative period.

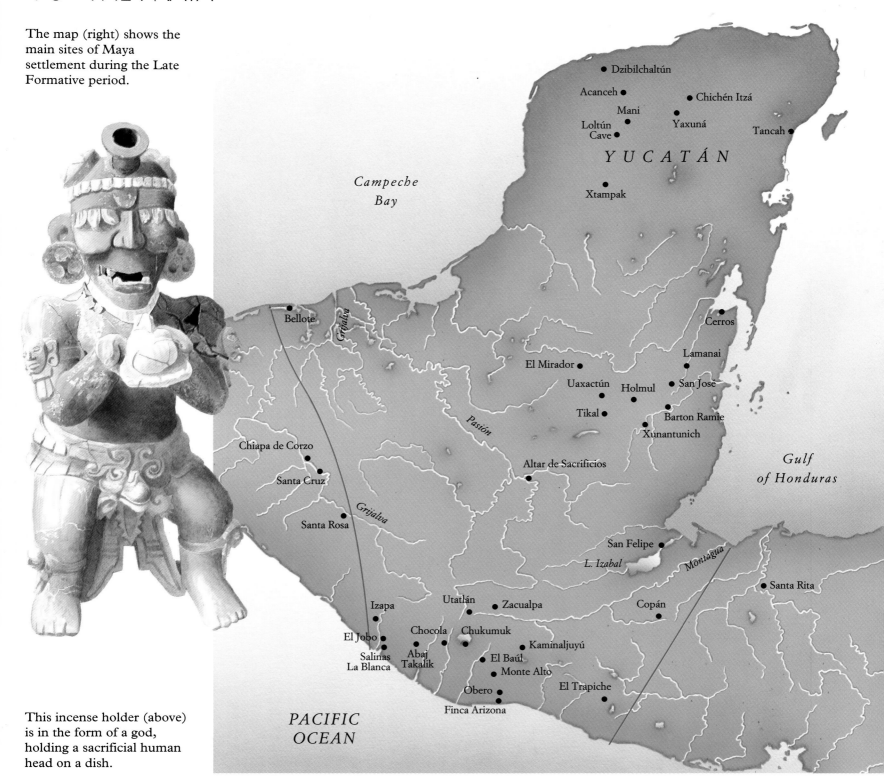

This incense holder (above) is in the form of a god, holding a sacrificial human head on a dish.

Campeche Bay

Bellote

Grijalva

Grijalva

Pasión

YUCATÁN

• Dzibilchaltún

Acanceh •
Mani
Loltún • • Yaxuná
Cave •
Xtampak •

• Chichén Itzá

Tancah •

• Cerros

• Lamanai

El Mirador •
Uaxactún • Holmul • San José
Tikal • • Barton Ramie
Xunantunich •

• Altar de Sacrificios

Chiapa de Corzo •

Santa Cruz •

Santa Rosa •

Gulf of Honduras

San Felipe •
L. Izabal
Montagua

• Santa Rita

Izapa •
El Jobo •
Salinas
La Blanca
Abaj
Takalik
Chocola •
Chukumuk •
Obero •
Finca Arizona

Utatlán • • Zacualpa
• Kaminaljuyú
• El Baúl
• Monte Alto
• El Trapiche

• Copán

PACIFIC OCEAN

The male figure (right) comes from Jaina, Campeche state, Mexico, and dates from the Upper Classic period.

The jade disc (below) has Mayan writing on it and is shown in detail on page 43.

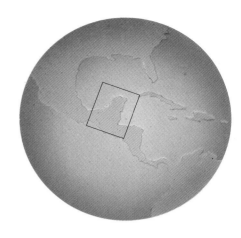

The battle scene (below) shows a Mayan city under attack. The enemy warriors are trying to cross the ditch using pole-bridges, but still face the obstacle of the fence. Pyramid temples can be seen in the distance.

10 THE MAYA

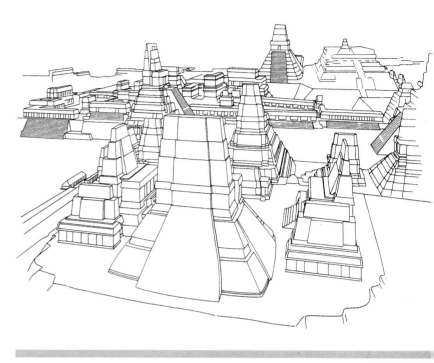

An artist's reconstruction of the city of Tikal (below).

Historians do not know if the Maya were the direct descendants of ancient groups of hunter-gatherers or of outsiders, who moved into lands in and around the Yucatán peninsula after settlement had begun there. It seems that the languages belonging to the Mayan group had developed by about 2500 BC. Scholars have split the Mayan culture into four main periods. They are known as Archaic (about 7000 to 2000 BC); Pre-Classic or Formative (about 2000 BC to AD 199); Classic (199 to about 900); and Post-Classic (up to the Spanish conquest of 1523-1541). The precise date of the Classic Period comes from an inscription on a stone known as the Hauberg Stele, the oldest Mayan inscription so far deciphered.

The civilization of the Maya
The Mayan civilization was one of the richest in all the Americas. The Maya lived in what are today Mexico, Guatemala, Belize, parts of Honduras and El Salvador. They were originally a mountain people, living in highlands rich in minerals such as obsidian, jade, serpentine and cinnabar, but also with temperate valleys and well-watered plateaus. Sites of importance were Izapa and Kaminaljuyú. Izapa, near the Pacific coast, shows Olmec influence and was occupied until the Late Formative period. Kaminaljuyú was on the western fringes of modern Guatemala, and arose at the start of the Classic period.

The Mayan civilization flourished in the southern lowlands, where rainforest was thick (modern Honduras, Belize, Guatemala, and the states of Chiapas and Tabasco in Mexico), and this is where the major sites are. Later, during the Post-Classic period, these lowlands were abandoned, and Mayan culture lingered on only in the north of Yucatán, an inhospitable region of heat and swamp.

How the Maya lived
The Maya lived in more than 50 politically independent regions, the largest of which was possibly Tikal. Each region had a capital city and smaller towns, but most people lived in villages. Whole families lived together, sharing not only blood-ties but also their own special skills or trades. Each city-state had its own ruler, who was a god-king. When he died, power passed to a close relative, usually a son or brother. The king chose nobles known as cahels to rule subordinate towns and districts.

The king received tribute from his subjects in the form of

This view of Copán (pictured in colour on pages 40/41) shows one of the great Mayan cities in the south. It stood on the banks of the Copán river in Honduras. The royal dynasty that ruled the city was founded in AD 426, and a line of 16 kings ruled for 400 years thereafter.

The city was at its most splendid in the AD 600s, when its area was about 39 sq km (15 sq miles). Today, only ruins remain of its huge temples. There are more than 30 stelae, or tall stones, the tallest of which is 3.5 metres (11.5 ft) high. These have pictures of the city rulers on them.

People climbed the Stairs of Hieroglyphics to reach the Temple of Inscriptions. The stairs contain the longest-known Mayan inscription, of 2,500 glyphs, or signs, written on 63 steps. The people shown in these inscriptions carry insignia marking their rank in society, but no weapons: there

are no scenes of war either.

The low building in the middle of the great plaza is the ball court. The game played here was more than just a fast, exciting spectacle. It was also a sacred rite, where the ball stood for the Sun and the court stood for the Earth.

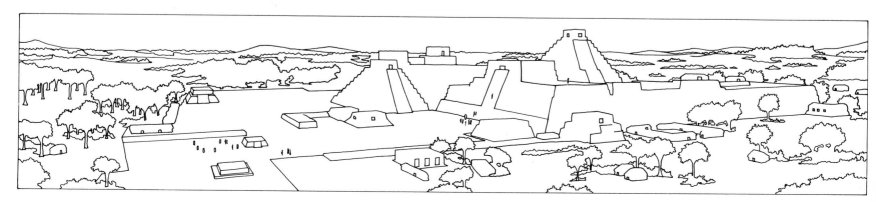

Mayan writing (above) had about 700 signs, which stood for pictures and sounds. Only about 250 of these have so far been deciphered.

One of the standing stones at Copán (left). It was drawn by George Catherwood, whose illustrations brought the wonders of Mayan culture to the world in the mid-19th century. Pictured on the stone is a ruler.

This chart (right) shows the Mayan number system, which was based on 20, and written with just three symbols: a stylized shell (0), a dot (1) and a bar (5).

The drawing (below) is of the inscribed jade disc (see pages 40-41) found at Pomona Ranch, Belize. The disc is 18 cm (7 in) across and shaped like an earring. Its symbols are read clockwise. On the left is the Sun God, with an inscription in a Mayan dialect called Yucatec. The Sun God is master of the number 4. Next comes the God of Darkness, then the God of Corn, lord of the number 8.

0	1	2
3	4	5
6	7	8
9	10	11
12	13	14
15	16	17

goods, food or services, such as labour to build temples and roads. He also controlled trade in the most sought-after products such as obsidian, cacao and cotton. He organized the larger agricultural schemes, which involved terracing hillsides, digging irrigation canals and cutting back the jungle as it encroached on to farmland.

Trade and the city

The Maya had no beasts of burden, and did not use the wheel on carts. Nevertheless, they had a busy road and river network, along which traders travelled as far as the Gulf coast, to the territory of the Zapotecs and Teotihuacáns.

Life centred on the city, which was the heart of Mayan power and religion. Public buildings were decorated with relief sculptures and wall paintings, which were used by the rulers to celebrate royal triumphs, list family trees, and link the king with the all-powerful gods. The temples themselves, at first modest buildings, evolved into massive complexes on high platforms, with pyramid-temples, palaces, astronomical observatories, courts for playing the ball-game (which had a religious significance), and wide open squares, or plazas.

Writing and numbers

The Maya wrote in hieroglyphs, or picture-signs, which also represented sounds. Their number system was based on 20, and included the concept of 0 (zero), used in the Old World only by the Babylonians and Hindus, and not used in Europe before the Middle Ages. The Mayan calendar had 260 days for the ceremonial/religious year, and 365 days for the civil year, divided into 18 months of 20 days each.

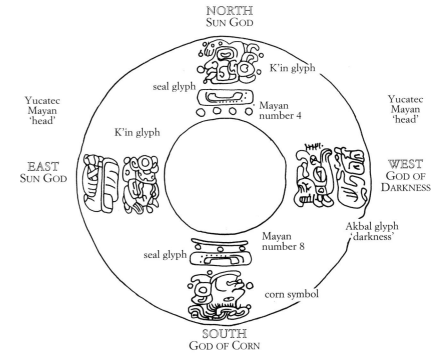

The picture (below) is of the Rabbit-God, posing as a scribe writing a manuscript. The Maya wrote on strips of bark glued and folded like a concertina, then bound in jaguar skin.

43

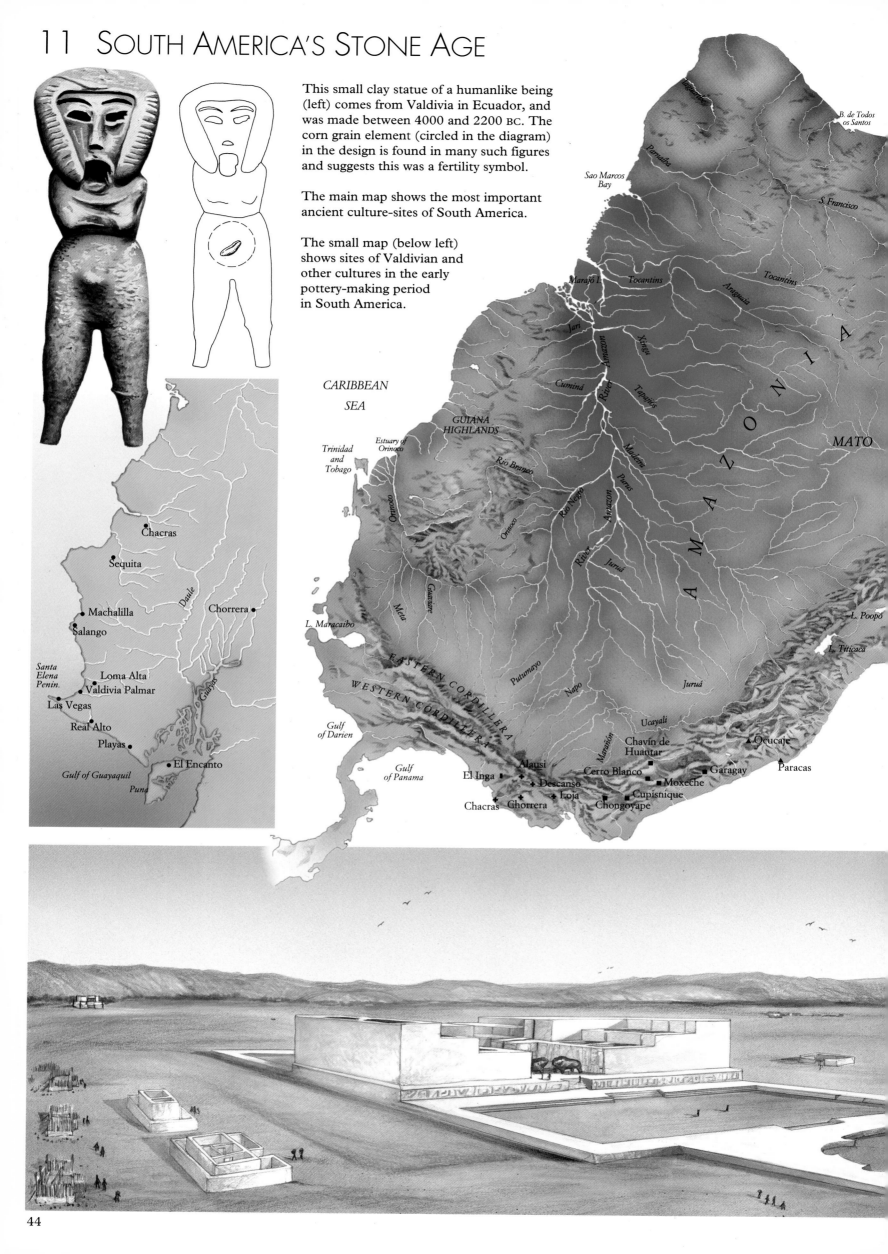

This small clay statue of a humanlike being (left) comes from Valdivia in Ecuador, and was made between 4000 and 2200 BC. The corn grain element (circled in the diagram) in the design is found in many such figures and suggests this was a fertility symbol.

The main map shows the most important ancient culture-sites of South America.

The small map (below left) shows sites of Valdivian and other cultures in the early pottery-making period in South America.

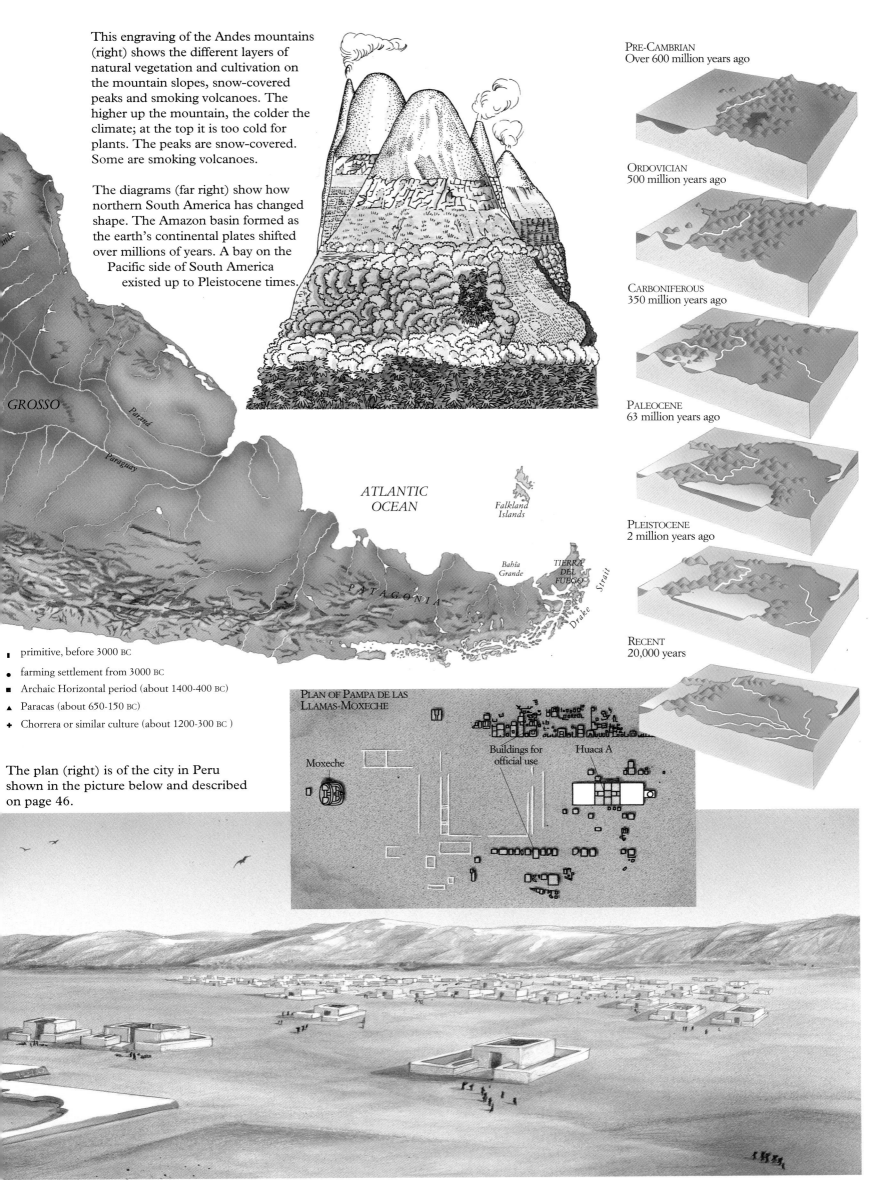

This engraving of the Andes mountains (right) shows the different layers of natural vegetation and cultivation on the mountain slopes, snow-covered peaks and smoking volcanoes. The higher up the mountain, the colder the climate; at the top it is too cold for plants. The peaks are snow-covered. Some are smoking volcanoes.

The diagrams (far right) show how northern South America has changed shape. The Amazon basin formed as the earth's continental plates shifted over millions of years. A bay on the Pacific side of South America existed up to Pleistocene times.

PRE-CAMBRIAN
Over 600 million years ago

ORDOVICIAN
500 million years ago

CARBONIFEROUS
350 million years ago

PALEOCENE
63 million years ago

PLEISTOCENE
2 million years ago

RECENT
20,000 years

GROSSO

Paraná

Paraguay

ATLANTIC OCEAN

Falkland Islands

Bahía Grande

TIERRA DEL FUEGO

Drake Strait

P A T A G O N I A

▪ primitive, before 3000 BC

● farming settlement from 3000 BC

■ Archaic Horizontal period (about 1400-400 BC)

▲ Paracas (about 650-150 BC)

✛ Chorrera or similar culture (about 1200-300 BC)

The plan (right) is of the city in Peru shown in the picture below and described on page 46.

PLAN OF PAMPA DE LAS LLAMAS-MOXECHE

Moxeche

Buildings for official use

Huaca A

45

This pottery jar (left) was made by people of Chavín de Huantar, who lived in what are now Peru and Bolivia. It shows a dead person, and was perhaps a funerary vessel.

South America has a simpler and more extreme geography than North America. On the west coast the Pacific Ocean washes one of the most arid desert coasts in the world; on the east is the vast Amazon basin, with its huge river systems and luxuriant rainforest. The Andes Mountains, one of the greatest mountain ranges on earth, stretch from north to south, down to the wind-scoured plains of Tierra del Fuego.

South America has four main areas. First is the Intermediate and Caribbean region, which includes the Caribbean islands, parts of Venezuela, Ecuador and Colombia, and what are now Nicaragua, Costa Rica and Panama in Central America. Then there is the Andes region, with Peru and Bolivia in the centre, and Chile and Argentina to the south. The remaining regions are Amazonia and the southernmost area of Patagonia.

The first human settlements
About 3000 BC, as the Paleolithic, or Old Stone Age, gave way to the Neolithic, or New Stone Age, the southern half of the New World experienced an advance in human culture. South America was populated late in prehistoric terms, as people moved south across the isthmus of Panama from North America. Yet the picture is not so clear as once appeared, for similar developments seem to have been taking place in both North and South America at roughly the same time. There was much contact between the peoples of Mesoamerica and those farther south, especially in Ecuador, which was a meeting-point for trade. There are signs of Ecuadorian influence on clothing, pit tombs and grave goods among peoples living in the north.

Water was all-important to these early South Americans. They needed water for farming, as populations grew and more food was required. To provide water, there were advanced irrigation systems. People living near mountain sources of stone used stone in their buildings and monuments, while people living beside the coasts where stone was scarce relied on adobe (sun-dried mud) as a building material. People perfected the making of textiles and pottery, and began to extract metals, such as gold, from the mountains and river beds.

Migrations
While the main flow of people was from north to south, there were other migrations. People from Venezuela crossed the Caribbean Sea to settle in the islands of the Antilles. This began about 2500 BC, although some islands had been settled much earlier, about 5000 BC. A second, more gradual, migration took place from the Orinoco region on the east coast between 1000 and 500 BC. These

The reconstruction below (pictured in colour on pages 44/45) shows the city of Pampa de las Llamas-Moxeche in Peru. This city grew up between 2200 and 1100 BC on a flat plain about 350 km (217 miles) north of modern Lima. The settlement was large, consisting of about a dozen minor centres grouped around the main

ceremonial site. Here there were temples up to 30 metres (98 ft) high and bigger than a football pitch, like the Moxeche temple shown below.

Smaller buildings, square-shaped with walls around them, faced an even bigger building known as Huaca A. This was in two identical halves. It looks like a

warehouse and probably was a storehouse for cereals and trade goods, offered to the gods. People climbed huge stairways to get in, passing great jaguar-like statues which were meant to frighten away intruders.

The city itself consisted of smaller houses grouped together, as shown in the background of the

picture. This neat planning is further evidence of the sophistication of these comparatively little-known South American civilizations. The main building materials were adobe bricks, and blocks of granite faced with softer limestone.

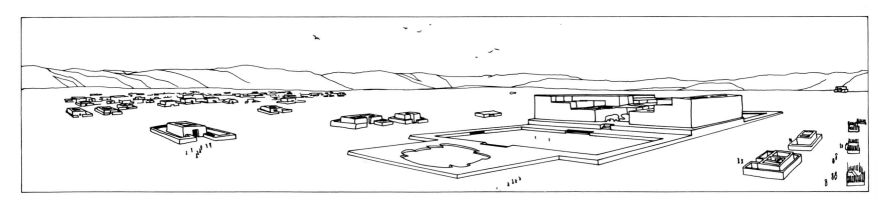

Skilled weavers created elaborate costumes, like this cloak (left) worn by an important person of the Paracas people of Peru.

The condor is often shown in Andean art. This condor (left) has a snake on its breast, and was made by dyeing cotton cloth. It comes from northern Peru and dates from about 2000 BC.

migrants were the Arawak, who were hunter-gatherers as well as expert fishermen and canoe-sailors making voyages both for trade and to explore. They grew sweet potatoes and manioc, in addition to the staple Mesoamerican foods of corn, beans and squash. They lived in villages of bell-shaped huts, with thatched roofs.

Settling mainland South America

On the northern mainland of South America, people moved from hunting and gathering to agriculture about 2500 BC. They grew edible roots, such as manioc, and later corn. They fashioned huge slabs of stone such as those found at Gran Chiriqui, the purpose of which remains a mystery. In Costa Rica, corn grinders made from rectangular stones, often decorated, have been found, and in Colombia numerous masks have been discovered. But the most important goods made by these peoples were gold objects, such as those created by the Tairona goldsmiths, a community whose civilization reached its peak about AD 1000. They lived high in the Colombian mountains of the Sierra Nevada de Santa Marta, and the site known as Buritac 200 was an important trade centre, a town of gold miners and merchants who followed the trade routes that crossed at this point.

Little is known of how the Tairona people lived, but their society must have been quite complex to maintain such a level of skills. Another important site in Colombia is San Agustin, which is almost as high as Buritac, at 1,800 metres (5,905 ft) above sea level. Here there are burial mounds and pit tombs, raised platforms that may have been temples, irrigation canals, and many sculptures, which are in a style later common across the central Andes region.

This chart shows the main civilizations of South America's chief ancient settlement regions – the coast and the mountains, from the Stone Age to the Inca empire.

GOLDWORKING

Metalworking began in South America before 1500 BC, but the crafting of gold came later. The first finds date from about 800 BC. To begin with, the gold was simply rolled into sheets or leaves, and then cut or pressed to shape. Later it was melted and used to make casts. The South Americans became expert goldsmiths, especially the Colombians. They were able to combine cold and hot working, and to use alloys by mixing gold with silver and copper to obtain brilliant results. Gold was found abundantly in mountains and rivers. It was not regarded as having great commercial value in itself. Its importance lay in its symbolic associations with the gods and with the power of kings. South American gold objects include some of enormous richness, especially of decoration, intricately shaped. What we have today is only a fragment of the artistic wealth that once existed.

Period	Date	COAST			MOUNTAINS			
		NORTH	CENTRAL	SOUTH	NORTH	CENTRAL	SOUTH	FAR SOUTH
Horizontal III	1534 1463	Inca-Chimú	Inca	Inca	Inca-Cajamarca	Inca	Inca	Inca
Upper Intermediate Period	1000	Chimú	Chancay	Chincha	Cajamarca Huari	Huari	Pre-Inca	Aymara
Horizontal II	600	Mochica Huari	Pachacamac Huari	Pacheco-Huari	Huari Cajamarca III	Huari	Huari	Tiahuanaco IV
Intermediate lower period	AD 200 / 200 BC	Mochica Mochica and Virú	Kingdom of Lima Bono de Boza	Nazca Nazca-Paracas Necropolis	Cajamarca II Cajamarca and Recuay	Huari	Huari Pucará	Tiahuanaco III
Horizontal I	1200	Salinar-Virú Chavín	Tracce Chavín	Paracas Cavernas	Chavín	Chavín-Kotosh		Tiahuanaco I-II Tiahuanaco I
Early Upper	1800	Huaca Negra Las Aldas Huaca Prieta	La Florida Tranque site	Hatcha site		Kotosh IV Kotosh III		
Early Lower Pre-Ceramic	2500 3500 5000 6000 7000	Huaca Prieta Playa Culebras	Asia Paraiso-Rio Seco Chilca	Cabezas Largas		Kotosh II Kotosh I Lauricocha III Lauricocha II		
Upper Lithic	8000 11000	Chivateros II Chivateros I				Lauricocha I Guitarrero	Pikimachay	
Lower Lithic	12000 20000		Chivateros R.Z.				Pikimachay	

12 FIRST CIVILIZATIONS OF THE ANDES

The map (right) shows the first centres of civilization in the Andes. The development of agriculture brought a growth of population, as is shown by the increase in the number and size of settlements. People began to make goods such as pots, textiles and ornaments, for use in trade with their neighbours. In this way, too, cultures mingled.

The small map (below) shows the Galapagos Islands off the coast of Ecuador. The islands were visited in the early 1800s by the naturalist Charles Darwin, whose observations there were important to the study of evolution and human development.

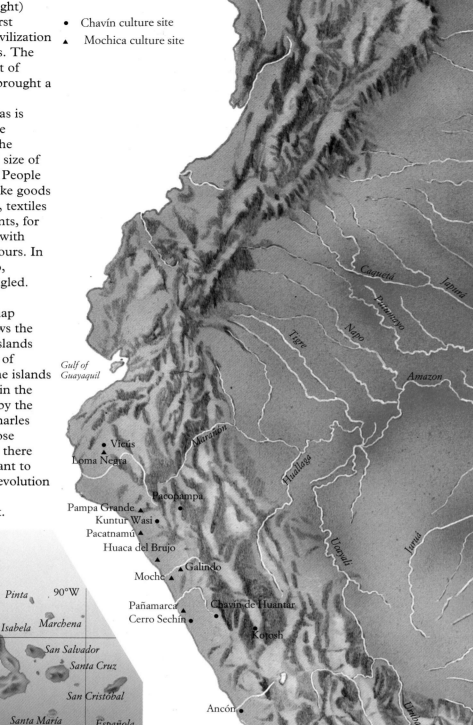

- • Chavín culture site
- ▲ Mochica culture site

This Nazca rock-picture (below) shows an animal, possibly a puma, as a kind of 'negative' image.

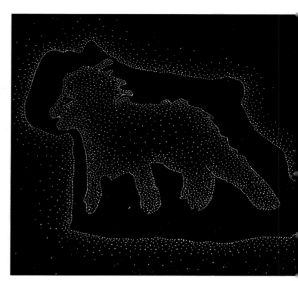

The two pictures (below) from Huayhua in Peru also Nazca reliefs: (a) shows human figures dressed for a ritual; (b) illustrates the myth of the Nazca sun-hero.

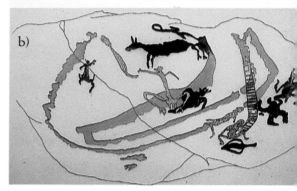

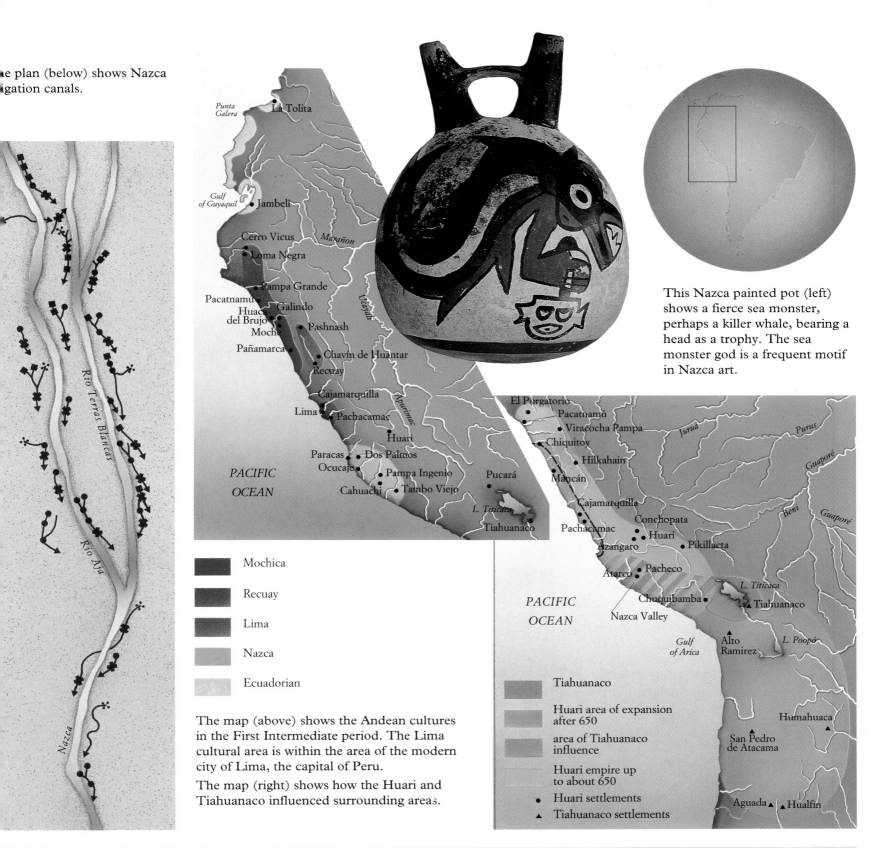

The plan (below) shows Nazca irrigation canals.

Punta Galera

La Tolita

Gulf of Guyaquil

Jambeli

Cerro Vicus

Loma Negra

Marañon

Pampa Grande

Pacatnamú

Galindo

Huaca del Brujo

Moche

Pashnash

Pañamarca

Chavín de Huantar

Recuay

Cajamarquilla

Lima

Pachacamac

Huari

Paracas

Dos Palmos

Ocucaje

Pampa Ingenio

Pucará

Cahuachi

Tambo Viejo

L. Titicaca

Tiahuanaco

PACIFIC OCEAN

Ucayali

Apurimac

Río Terras Blancas

Río Aja

Nazca

Mochica

Recuay

Lima

Nazca

Ecuadorian

The map (above) shows the Andean cultures in the First Intermediate period. The Lima cultural area is within the area of the modern city of Lima, the capital of Peru.

The map (right) shows how the Huari and Tiahuanaco influenced surrounding areas.

This Nazca painted pot (left) shows a fierce sea monster, perhaps a killer whale, bearing a head as a trophy. The sea monster god is a frequent motif in Nazca art.

El Purgatorio

Pacatnamú

Viracocha Pampa

Chiquitoy

Hilkahain

Mancán

Cajamarquilla

Conchopata

Pachacamac

Huari

Azangaro

Pikillacta

Atarco

Pacheco

Chuquibamba

Nazca Valley

L. Titicaca

Tiahuanaco

Alto Ramirez

Gulf of Arica

L. Poopó

Humahuaca

San Pedro de Atacama

Aguada

Hualfin

Jurua

Purus

Guaporé

Beni

Guaporé

PACIFIC OCEAN

Tiahuanaco

Huari area of expansion after 650

area of Tiahuanaco influence

Huari empire up to about 650

● Huari settlements

▲ Tiahuanaco settlements

12 FIRST CIVILIZATIONS OF THE ANDES

The civilizations of the Andes represent the second major cultural region of early America, after Mesoamerica. They were concentrated mainly along the Andes mountains in what is now Peru. Here the two main geographic areas were the Sierra or mountains, and the Coast, on the western side of the Andes.

As in Mesoamerica, people who had originally been semi-nomadic hunter-gatherers began to settle, to farm the land, to domesticate animals, and to fish. What historians call the Andean Formative period lasted from 2500 BC to AD 300, and during its first phase (2500 to 1500 BC) settlements of importance developed in the central Coastal region. These were El Paraóso, where people exploited the sea's resources for food; Huaca la Florida, inland, where farmers used simple but effective irrigation methods; Las Haldas, a town of 10,000 inhabitants; and Cerro Sechín, which had buildings of adobe and painted stone, where pictures of warriors and sacrificial victims have been found.

The Coastal peoples were able to find fish and shellfish to eat, but continued to hunt animals and gather plants, as well as growing crops. They traded with the peoples living in the mountains, where there were fewer settlements. Two of these were Kotosh and Pacopampa.

Farming and population growth
About 1000 BC farmers learned to grow corn, and the result was a food surplus which boosted the growth of civilization. This next phase of more advanced development is evidenced by the finds at Chavín de Huantar. This seems to have been a ceremonial centre, with a temple culture ruled by priests. It had a key strategic position, controlling trade routes, and was able to influence both the Coastal and Sierra peoples of northern Peru. Archaeologists have found inscribed stones, obelisk monuments, carved heads, animal sculptures (jaguars, snakes, condors, eagles) at Chavín. Nearer the coast, pottery, textiles, carved bones and gourds have been discovered.

A complex of religious centres developed in this region, all linked to the same cult. The keynote of Andean civilization was an economic system founded on the distribution of water to farmers, on trade, and on the payment of tribute to the temple priests, who were the effective rulers of the society. The chief gods seem to have been the jaguar-god, and the condor and snake.

As society developed, the priests lost some of their power to a new ruling class of warrior-nobles. Farming became more efficient, with larger irrigation schemes, and the population continued to grow steadily. Chavín influence extended to other centres, such as Paracas, Lima, Salinar and Virú.

The Mochica
The Mochica were a people living in northern Peru who developed a strong political federation. They made

The pictures below (shown in colour on pages 48/49) illustrate aspects of Nazca culture. The left-hand picture shows how these people built dams and reservoirs to store water for irrigation.

The people shown here are working to divert water from underground springs into canals. Such engineering works required considerable effort and organization from people whose tools were mostly made of stone. They needed to save as much water as they could for, living in the shadow of the Andes, they were in one of the driest regions of the American continent.

The right-hand picture shows one of the famous Nazca line-pictures in the desert. It is a gigantic spider. Some of the animal outlines are 300 metres (almost 1,000 ft) across. There are even bigger geometric patterns, up to 10 km (6.2 miles) long. Exactly how and why the Nazca made these pictures, which they could never see in total as dramatically as modern aerial photos reveal them, remains a mystery.

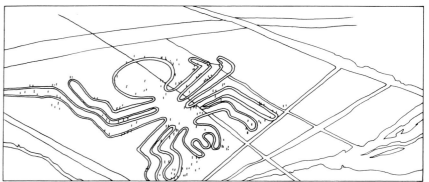

An artist's reconstruction (opposite) of archaeological excavations at Los Gavrilane in the coastal desert of Peru. People here stored corn in conical pits lined with stone. The pits were sealed with sand when filled. Llamas are used to help carry the harvest. This was before pottery was made, about 2800 BC.

This is the typical reed boat used on Lake Titicaca (right), a large lake more than 3,800 metres (12,500 ft) above sea level. Such craft are still used by local people to fish and travel across the lake.

This picture (right, below) was a decoration on a pot. It shows a Mochica warrior with a captive.

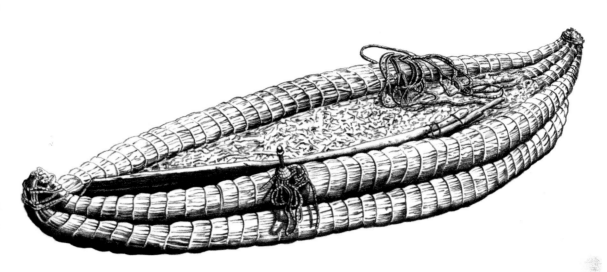

handsomely decorated pottery, and their style of building was based on the use of sun-dried clay bricks (adobe). Using these bricks, they built houses, and step pyramids as temples.

The Mochica diet was based on corn, potatoes, peppers, and the meat of llamas, guinea pigs and dogs. The people made cloth from cotton, and from the wool of the alpaca and vicuna produced the finest textiles in America. They also made objects in gold, silver and copper, although they never mastered bronzeworking.

The Nazca and their lines
On the southern coast of Peru there lived a people called the Nazca, whose culture was developed from that of Paracas. They made pots decorated with pictures of plants and animals, as well as abstract designs. Most remarkably, the Nazca also made pictures on the ground, creating outlines of stylized animals and birds so large that they can be seen clearly only from the air.

Tiahuanaco and Huari
Until the AD 500s these societies of the Andes region prospered, without much interference from outside and with little change in their form of government or economy. Around the first century AD, there arose on the banks of Lake Titicaca a new and powerful city-state known as Tiahuanaco. It had grown from one of the villages clustered around the lake and its people were farmers and traders. But by about 600, Tiahuanaco was losing its position as the first city of the Andes. In the central mountains of Peru was an expanding kingdom called Huari. Huari took in the old kingdom of the Mochica, but was also shaped by the traditions of Nazca and Tiahuanaco civilization. Its dominance lasted until about AD 1000, and its culture was copied in Peru, part of Bolivia and northern Chile.

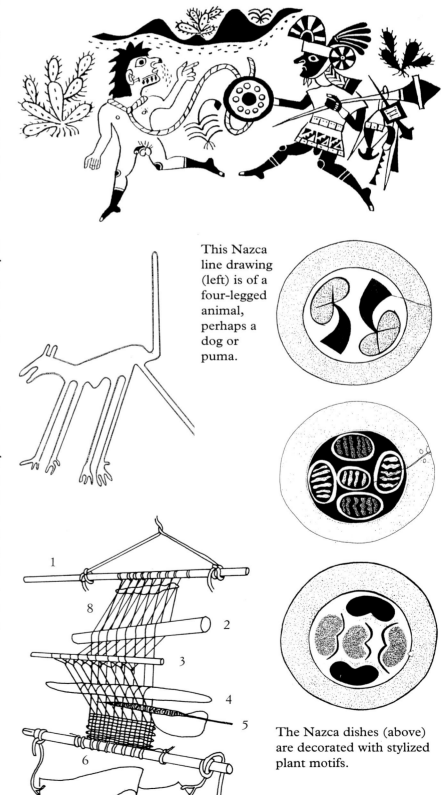

This Nazca line drawing (left) is of a four-legged animal, perhaps a dog or puma.

The Nazca dishes (above) are decorated with stylized plant motifs.

The Andean peoples were expert weavers of cloth. This is a diagram of the kind of loom they used. 1. frame support; 2. warp beam; 3. heddle; 4. beater; 5. shuttle with weft thread; 6. harness fastening; 7. weaver's belt; 8. warp threads.

from the darkly shaded forest floor, through the upper levels of thick growth, to the canopy through which the tallest trees reach up towards the sunlight.

The Kayapó people of the Amazon divide thé forest into ten levels, anticipating modern biologists in their knowledge of ecology and how nature organizes itself to take advantage of all environments. Like other forest peoples, the Kayapó developed a way of life that made use of the forest resources without threatening to destroy its plants and animals.

The Amazon forest is the richest and most complex ecosystem in the world. It has a wealth of plants – up to 600 species to each hectare (2.5 acres) – and in all more than 90,000 individual plant species grow there. The most dominant are the slender lianas. The forest plants occupy a series of layers,

The Amazon basin is the world's biggest river system. It covers an area greater than Europe, and scientists have called it the richest 'genetic reservoir' of species on earth. The human population of the Amazon was originally made up of about 1,000 tribal groups, numbering from two to three million people. Most of these people lived close to the rivers. They had more than 500 languages, belonging to 20 language families.

The map (below) shows the Amazon basin and the areas where the main tribal groups lived.

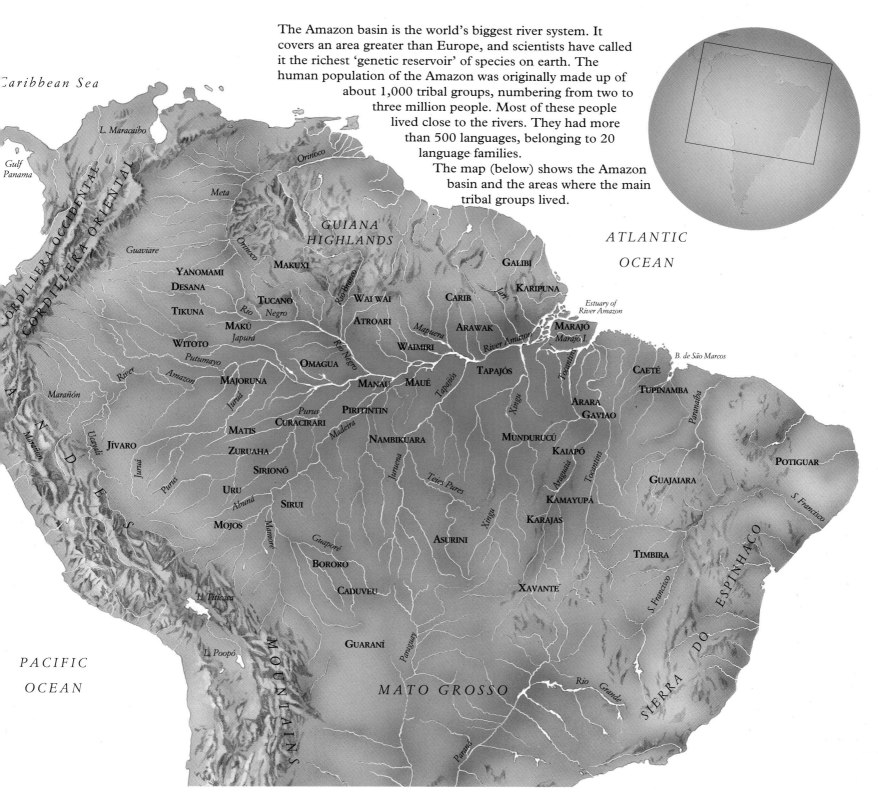

Caribbean Sea

Gulf Panama

L. Maracaibo

CORDILLERA OCCIDENTAL
CORDILLERA ORIENTAL

Guaviare

Meta

Orinoco

GUIANA HIGHLANDS

ATLANTIC OCEAN

YANOMAMI
DESANA
TIKUNA
MAKUXI
TUCANO
WAI WAI
CARIB
GALIBI
KARIPUNA

Rio Negro
Rio Branco

MAKÚ
WITOTO
OMAGUA
ATROARI
WAIMIRI
ARAWAK
MARAJÓ
Estuary of River Amazon
Marajó I.

Japurá
Putumayo
Río
Negro

Amazon
River
Marañón

MAJORUNA
MANAU
MAUÉ
TAPAJÓS
Mapuera
River Amazon
B. de São Marcos
CAETÉ

MATIS
CURACIRARI
PIRITINTIN
NAMBIKUARA
Madeira
Tapajós
Xingu
Tocantins
ARARA
GAVIAO
TUPINAMBA
Paranaíba

ZURUAHA
SIRIONÓ
URU
Juruena
MUNDURUCÚ
KAIAPÓ
Araguaia
Tocantins
GUAJAIARA
POTIGUAR
S. Francisco

JÍVARO
Ucayali
Juruá
Purus
Abuná
Teles Pures
KAMAYUPÁ
KARAJAS

SIRUI
Mamoré
ASURINI
Xingu
TIMBIRA

MOJOS
BORORO
CADUVEU
Guaporé
XAVANTE
S. Francisco

L. Titicaca

GUARANÍ
Paraguay

L. Poopó

PACIFIC OCEAN

MATO GROSSO
Rio Grande
SIERRA DO ESPINHAÇO

MOUNTAINS
ANDES
Marañón

Paraná

13 PEOPLES OF THE AMAZON

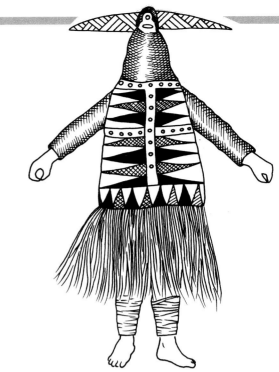

A ritual funeral mask and costume of a Tucano chief.

The Amazon basin is immense. Flowing across it is the longest river in South America, the Amazon, fed by many tributaries. The natural vegetation is a very dense tropical forest, the biggest on earth and the richest in plant species, with trees towering 45 metres (147 ft) or more above the forest floor. Scientists have calculated that the Amazon contains at least a third of all the earth's plant species, and the forest also has an extraordinarily wide array of animals.

The most fertile areas are the narrow plains either side of the rivers, which are flooded every year. In the forest, humidity is very high, as much as 80 per cent, making life for humans difficult. Not surprisingly, the first people to reach here, who were hunter-gatherers, stayed close to the rivers, making only forays into the forest.

When people first arrived in the Amazon

At the site of Lagoa Santa, archaeologists have found human skeletons and bones of now-extinct animals, and although dating is imprecise as yet, it is thought that the first people in the Amazon region arrived there by 10,000 BC. Numerous finds from about 6500 BC have been made in the same area: shell necklaces, bone tools, finely shaped stones, arrows with stone heads, and bone instruments used for hunting. The damp, hot conditions of the forest quickly decay organic materials, so that most of the evidence of early humans has been lost.

Contacts with other peoples

The theory is that there were two main avenues for the cultural exchanges between the Amazon and the surrounding regions. There is evidence of some contact with Andean cultures, spreading slowly from west to east as far as the island of Marajó at the mouth of the Amazon. The second route for cultural transmission was from Venezuela, by way of the Orinoco and Amazon rivers.

Phases of Amazon culture

Amazon cultures developed in three phases. First, people who were hunters and gatherers turned to farming, probably learning the skills from contact with more advanced western cultures. They later began to make pottery, again following Andean models. In the second phase, people found that growing crops was preferable to hunting, and they began a slash-and-burn system of forest cultivation – clearing a patch of forest by burning the trees, planting crops until the soil was exhausted, and then moving on after a few years. This new way of life made people more settled, and able to develop simple but more organized social structures. They began building different styles of dwellings, for different uses. The pottery made in the first

In the scene (pictured in colour on pages 52/53) Amazon Indian hunters seek game in the forest. They are expert hunters, using the blowpipe and poison-tipped arrows to kill small animals such as monkeys and birds. Their target here is a sloth, one of the many unique creatures of the rainforest. The bird on the left of the picture is a toucan.

The hunters wear little clothing, and everything they use in their daily lives they make or find in the forest. The forest has many dangers even for its own people. Jaguars prowl the riverside, and in the water caimans and large anaconda snakes lie half-hidden. Smaller, but even more dangerous, are the voracious piranha fish. There are poisonous insects, and myriad biting mosquitoes and flies.

But the forest people know and respect the animal inhabitants of the forest. They recognize its many species of plants, choosing some to eat and others to use as medicines or to induce trancelike states during shamanistic rituals. They are at home in the vast forest.

This figure (left) of a human/animal is made of terracotta and was found in the forest of Bolivia. It dates from between the 3rd and 2nd millennia BC.

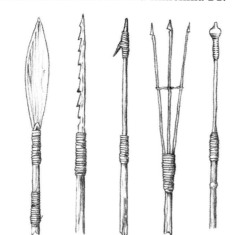

These drawings (left) show various kinds of arrows used by Amazon hunters.

Tucano and Nambikuara

Pano and Xiriana

Tupian

Arawak

Macro Ge

Carib

The Amazonian hut had a symbolic shape, with different parts of the dwelling having special significance.

The diagram (top) shows how the hut was partitioned into sections with their own functions. The central area was given over to collective ceremonial rituals, and the corner near to the men's entrance was kept for visitors and guests staying in the house. The hut was seen as a 'body', with male and female entrances associated with bodily functions (breathing/speech and so on).

The diagram (bottom) shows a 'womb-house'. It had a central space for ritual use, representing the foetus in the womb. The elements of fertility and procreation (male seed, menstrual blood) were present symbolically in the hut design.

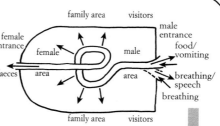

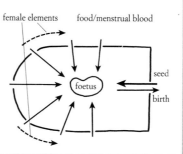

millennium AD seems to have been derived from Colombian models, which reached the Amazon by way of trade along the Orinoco.

The third phase is considered to be the most complex. Between 1200 and 1300, people developed a new and efficient social system, based on a more intensive type of farming, such as that in Central America. But this was a short-lived stage. Intensive farming failed to take root in the Amazon forest, probably because the climate and soils were unsuitable. People went back to the older slash-and-burn farming method, which gave them a livelihood but only at the expense of severe damage to the forest as the numbers of people farming in this wasteful way grew.

Many languages, one way of life

The Arawak were one of the most prominent forest peoples, whose language was for a long time the most widely spoken in the Amazon region. This language was also spoken in the Caribbean islands, where the Arawak peoples were driven out between 1000 and 500 BC. The Arawak were one of many groups in the Amazon. Though they spoke many languages, the forest peoples had much in common. They lived in small villages. There were village chiefs, and tribal chiefs who had authority over several villages. They worshipped gods and spirits who, they believed, controlled crops and the life cycles of animals and plants.

The maps (right) show the location of eight of the 500 or so language groups in the Amazon region. Originally, some 2 to 3 million people in 1,000 tribes lived here, in a land bigger than Europe.

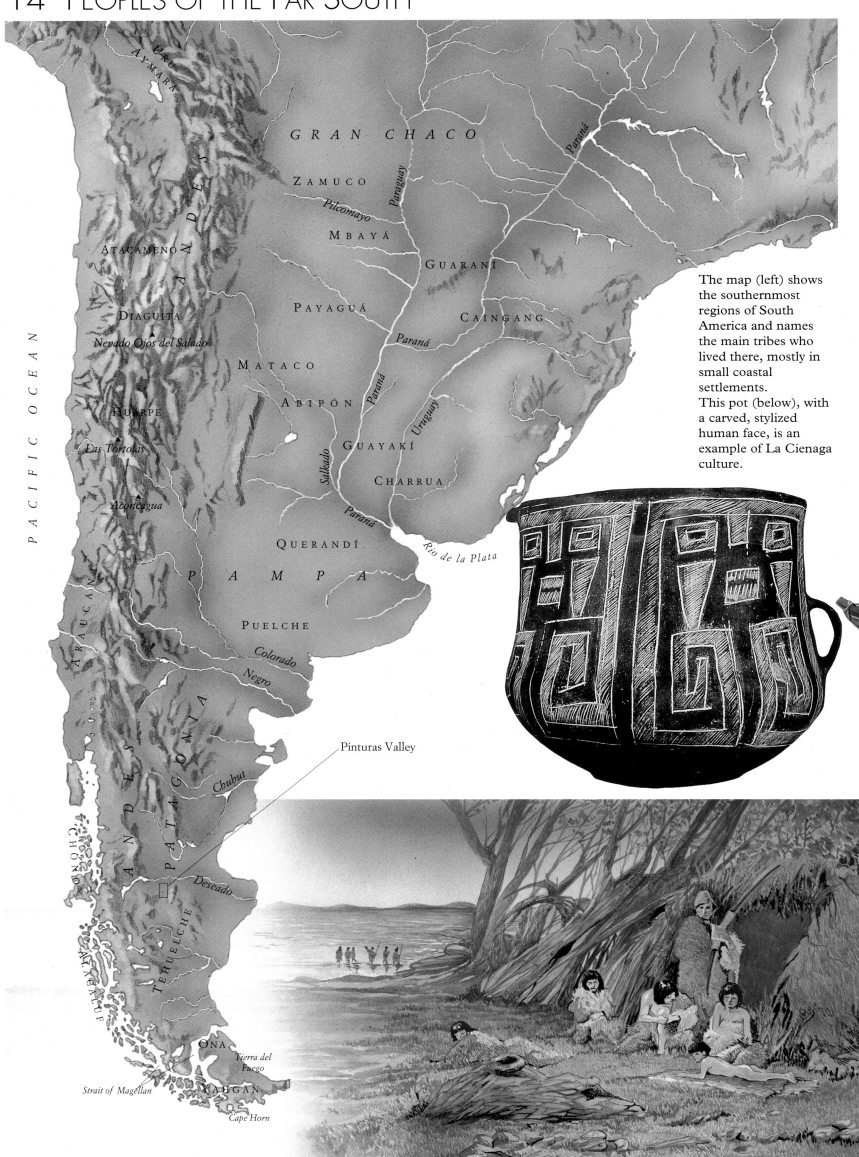

PACIFIC OCEAN

URU
AYMARA

GRAN CHACO

ZAMUCO

Pilcomayo

MBAYÁ

Paraguay

GUARANÍ

ATACAMEÑO

PAYAGUÁ

CAINGANG

DIAGUITA

Nevado Ojos del Salado

Paraná

MATACO

HUARPE

ABIPÓN

Las Tortolas

Parana

GUAYAKÍ

Uruguay

CHARRUA

Aconcagua

Salkado

QUERANDÍ

Paraná

Rio de la Plata

P A M P A

ARAUCAN

PUELCHE

Colorado

Negro

PATAGONIA

ANDES

Chubut

Pinturas Valley

CHONOS

Deseado

TEHUELCHE

ALAGALUF

ONA

Tierra del Fuego

Strait of Magellan

YAHGAN

Cape Horn

The map (left) shows the southernmost regions of South America and names the main tribes who lived there, mostly in small coastal settlements.
This pot (below), with a carved, stylized human face, is an example of La Cienaga culture.

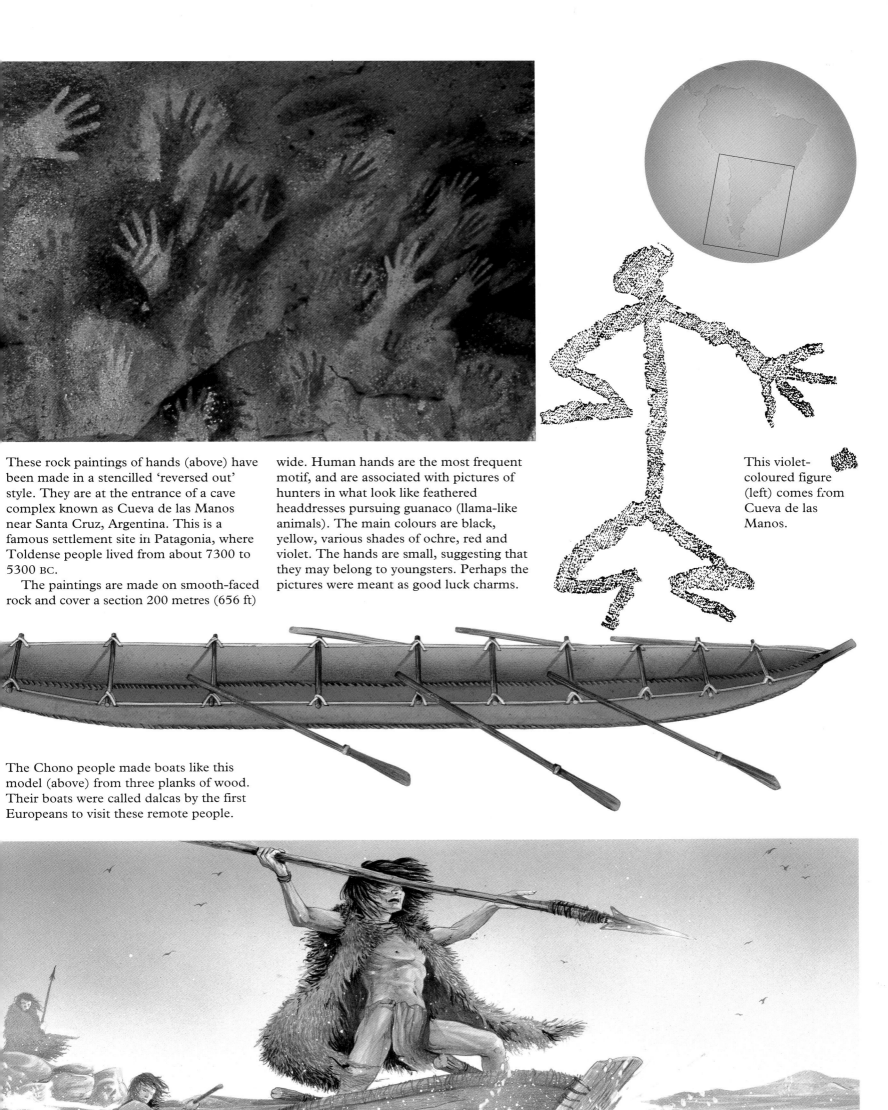

These rock paintings of hands (above) have been made in a stencilled 'reversed out' style. They are at the entrance of a cave complex known as Cueva de las Manos near Santa Cruz, Argentina. This is a famous settlement site in Patagonia, where Toldense people lived from about 7300 to 5300 BC.

The paintings are made on smooth-faced rock and cover a section 200 metres (656 ft) wide. Human hands are the most frequent motif, and are associated with pictures of hunters in what look like feathered headdresses pursuing guanaco (llama-like animals). The main colours are black, yellow, various shades of ochre, red and violet. The hands are small, suggesting that they may belong to youngsters. Perhaps the pictures were meant as good luck charms.

This violet-coloured figure (left) comes from Cueva de las Manos.

The Chono people made boats like this model (above) from three planks of wood. Their boats were called dalcas by the first Europeans to visit these remote people.

14 PEOPLES OF THE FAR SOUTH

This picture of a guanaco (below) is a detail from a rock painting at Cueva de las Manos in Santa Cruz province, Argentina.

The southernmost region of South America is the strip of land that is now within southern Chile and Argentina, including Patagonia and Tierra del Fuego. The culture of the people of this remote region extended to the islands of western Chile, as far as Chiloé.

The earliest human settlement in Patagonia has been located at Estancia Los Toldos, in the province of Santa Cruz in Argentina. The settlement, dated to about 12,600 years ago, has yielded one-edged stone tools flaked from larger stones, including razors. These are known as Toldense tools. Other finds include remains of the foods eaten by hunters: guanaco, an extinct llama, and an extinct horse known as *Parahipparion*.

About 200 km (124 miles) west of Estancia Los Toldos, in the Pinturas River region, there are other settlement sites such as Cueva de las Manos and Cueva Grande. These were inhabited later, from about 9,300 to 7,300 years ago. But the Toldense culture persisted.

Hunters with the bolas

About 5300 BC there arose a more advanced stone-tool culture, known as Casapedrense. Hunters now used the bolas, the typical throwing weapon of the South American plains. Later, from about 2500 BC, Patagonian peoples began making more sophisticated weapons and tools. Their way of life was still based on hunting guanaco, which provided the most important source of meat, hides and sinews. Pottery and the bow and arrow were not known until comparatively recent times, possibly about AD 700.

The Chono boat-people

At the southern tip of South America there are hundreds of islands and inlets. This was the home of the Chono, a people who shared a similar way of life, although originally they probably came from different groups. Their unique way of life persisted until the 1800s. The name Chono means 'southern boatmen'. They lived close to the ocean, in conditions very hostile to comfortable habitation, with scarce resources. Few traces are left of their culture, and what we know comes from reports by travellers and seamen.

The Chono lived as hunter-gatherers, relying heavily on the sea for food and making their camps on islands. They buried their dead in caves or ravines, and moved from island to island in canoes known as dalcas. These craft were made from three shaped planks of wood fastened together. On their journeys, the people took great care to keep a small fire burning in a clay hearth, to be transferred to their

Life in Tierra del Fuego (seen in colour on pages 56/57) was extremely hard. In a bleak land with a harsh climate, people live in shelters made from guanaco skins stretched over wooden poles. On rare sunny days, the skins can be drawn back, but mostly the shelter is tightly fastened against wind and rain. The family group travels between islands and coves in their boats. They wear only loincloths and guanaco skins, greased with fat on the inside to keep out the rain. Men, women and children sleep naked on the wet, cold ground. They have no shoes.

They spend their time gathering shellfish and fish trapped by the falling tide, and also hunt seabirds. Sometimes they are fortunate enough to come across the carcase of a dead seal or whale.

When they take to the sea, they brave rough seas and freezing cold water to hunt sealions. Their weapons are long, stone-tipped harpoons, and their craft are the slender, flat-bottomed boats that they fashion themselves from wood and animal sinews. To survive like this, people must indeed be tough.

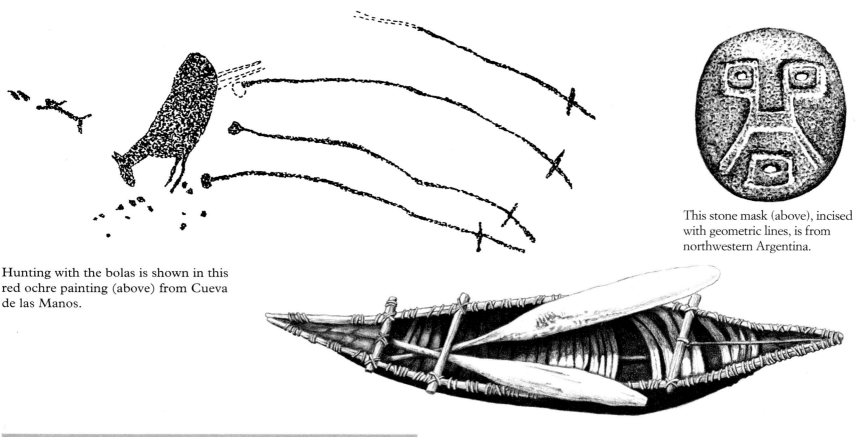

Hunting with the bolas is shown in this red ochre painting (above) from Cueva de las Manos.

This stone mask (above), incised with geometric lines, is from northwestern Argentina.

new camp when they landed.

The Chono caught fish, hunted sealions (from the fat of which they made a drink), and collected seaweed, which they made into weatherproof cloaks. Their chief food was shellfish, gathered by women who waded into the sea, where they also caught fish trapped in tidal pools. Occasionally a beached whale would be slaughtered. With no knowledge of preserving food, the Chono kept on the move to find new shellfish stocks. On dry land, they did a little farming, and built temporary shelters of tree bark.

Other peoples, and their fate

Another group of coastal people, the Alacaluf and Yahgan, lived in Tierra del Fuego. They too were boatmen, like the Chono. Inland lived the Fuegans, who gathered plants and hunted guanaco and foxes, eating the meat and using the skins to make cloaks and bags. They kept domesticated dogs. The Fuegans were also nomadic, and their homes were rough huts made from animal skins and shreds of bark spread across a framework of poles.

These southern peoples never developed pottery or weaving, and lacked such basic hunter-gatherer items as spear-throwers, axes or cooking pots. In Patagonia, to the north of Tierra del Fuego, there was a greater degree of social and technological advance. Here there were wide grasslands, home to the Puelche and Tehuelche. These people roamed in bands numbering from 50 to 150, led by a chief chosen for his skill as a hunter. They hunted guanaco, foxes and other animals, using stone tools and weapons, and lived in tents. Although they made baskets and engraved-bone objects, only a few groups progressed to making clay pots.

All these southern peoples were regarded as objects of curiosity by the first European explorers to come across them. They did not long survive contact with civilization, and had practically died out by the end of the 19th century.

This boat (above) and hunting weapons were found on Englefield Island, southern Chile. The weapons (right) include harpoons and stone points.

These are bolas stones (right). The stones were fastened to the ends of a thong or rope. The hunter whirled the bolas around his head before hurling it at the prey to stun it or bring it down.

This ceremonial axe (above) was made of bronze, and is of fairly late date. It comes from northwestern Argentina.

GLOSSARY

1 In this picture a hunter carries a spear-thrower, the spears he uses for hunting, and a bag for the kill. This rock painting was discovered in the Sao Raimundo Nonato region of northeastern Brazil.

2 A rock mask, from Teotihuacán. The rock is smoothed and polished and the eyes are made from beads of obsidian. The mask was photographed in Great Temple Museum in Mexico City.

adobe brick made of sun-hardened clay, or a building made from bricks of this type.

amulet a charm worn by people to keep off evil.

Archaic ancient, a term used by historians to describe the earliest period of a cycle of civilization growth.

ball-game game in some ways similar to the modern games of pelota and basketball, which was played by the peoples of Mesoamerica on a court with walls and hoops. The ball-game seems to have had important religious significance.

bas-relief type of sculpture in which the figures cut in the rock stand out slightly from the background.

bureaucracy officials who run the government of a state, region or city; the civil service.

caribou North American reindeer. Animals that migrate each year to find fresh grazing, and were hunted by ancient peoples.

clan families related to one another through a common ancestor.

condor a vulture and the largest flying bird, found in the mountains of California and South America.

corn maize or sweetcorn, one of the most important cereal crops in America.

desertification process caused by climatic changes that leads to the drying up of once-fertile land and the formation of new semi-desert and desert areas, with major consequences for people and animals.

domestication process by which people tamed wild animals such as cattle, horses and dogs to live alongside humans. Early peoples domesticated animals for food and as hunting companions. They also domesticated wild plants such as wheat and rice.

dynasty series of rulers descending in direct line from the original founder; a family of kings.

flint hard sedimentary rock, which was widely used for making stone tools and weapons because it splits and flakes when struck, producing sharp edges for cutting, piercing and scraping.

glaciation period of intense cold, during the Ice Ages, when glaciers covered large areas of the northern hemisphere, including Europe and North America.

glyph rock picture or writing made by cutting into the rock.

guanaco animal related to the camel, and similar in appearance to the llama; hunted by early peoples for its meat and wool.

harpoon missile weapon similar to a spear or lance, used for hunting seals and whales. The tip of the harpoon is barbed, to hold fast in the body of the prey. The harpoon was often fastened to a line so that the hunter could attach a float or haul in the wounded animal.

hierarchy social rank or order of importance of people within a group.

hieroglyphs form of writing made up of ideograms (picture-signs) and phonetic signs (signs standing for sounds).

indigenous native to or belonging to a place: indigenous people are the local people.

intensive farming farming carried on in a specialized way, using techniques such as irrigation and fertilizers and also tools to grow the heaviest crops possible.

irrigation watering farmland by means of wells, ditches and canals, to enable farmers to grow crops on land that would otherwise be too dry.

jade green or grey stone soft enough to be carved into intricate objects.

jaguar large spotted cat of Central and South America, revered by some peoples as a god-symbol.

lithic means 'of stone'; a megalith is a large block of stone, standing singly or in groups to form monuments.

llama animal related to the camel; it lives in South America and is a domesticated relative of the guanaco. People domesticated the llama as a pack animal.

mica mineral that splits easily into thin sheets.

3 The running animals are sheep or wild goats, with a deer behind. The small animal in the middle may be a hunting dog. This is a stone picture, perhaps Shoshone in origin, from the Coso mountain district of southeastern California.

4 This dyed fibre basket was made in the Cibola region of New Mexico (United States) and is now in the Chamber of Commerce Museum, Grants, New Mexico.

migration movement of people, either seasonally to find food, or from one territory to another to find new permanent homes.

Mongoloid describes people belonging to one of the three traditional racial groups (Caucasian, Negroid, Mongoloid) identified by their physical appearance. Mongoloid people came to America from Asia.

monochrome decoration using only one colour.

monopoly control of the sale and distribution of one item by a particular group of people, usually the producers of it.

Neolithic New Stone Age, a period of prehistory characterized by the spread of farming and animal-rearing, the invention of pottery and the making of polished stone tools.

nephrite mineral that is the chief source of jade. The states of Wyoming and Alaska have deposits of nephrite.

nomad person who moves from place to place, with no permanent home. Prehistoric hunter-gatherers were nomads, seeking fresh food sources. Early farmers were often semi-nomadic (part-nomads), moving on to new land when they had exhausted the soil in one place.

obsidian black glassy rock, highly valued by prehistoric people because it was sharp (for making knives) and highly decorative (for ceremonial objects and jewellery).

plaza Spanish for 'square' or open place in a city.

point stone tool made by shaping chips of flint to a sharp-tipped point.

potlatch festival of gift-giving or the gift itself, practised by the Native Americans of the Northwest.

Pre-Cambrian geological time period making up the first four million years of the Earth's history.

ritual religious ceremony, performed according to traditional rules.

sacrifice offering gifts to the gods to win their favour or appease their anger. Such gifts might be flowers, food, slaughtered animals or even slaughtered humans.

sedentary staying in one place, having a fixed place to live.

serpentine soft mineral, usually green.

shaman person believed to have magical powers through contacts with the spirit-world. Sometimes known as a 'medicine man', the shaman was a priest, healer, soothsayer and tribal wise man.

shellfish molluscs such as mussels, clams and oysters, which formed an important part of the diet of people living near rivers and sea coasts.

spear-thrower device used for throwing a spear over a greater distance; it had the effect of 'lengthening the arm' of the hunter as he threw his spear, and was known as an atlatl in America.

squash family of vegetables similar to pumpkins, widely grown in the Americas.

steatite mineral also known as soapstone, a kind of grey-green stone which is so soft that it has a soapy feel.

stele stone slab with inscriptions commemorating a dead person or an important event, or with some important message or laws written on it.

tectonic having to do with the shifting of rocky plates that form the Earth's crust; these movements alter the position and shape of the continents.

textiles materials made by weaving plant fibres (such as cotton) or animal fibres (such as wool).

totem comes from an Algonquin word meaning 'central sign', a representation of symbols (animals, plants, natural phenomena) with which people believe they have particular and traditional kinship. Typically a pole with painted carvings of animal and human-like heads.

trance state of unconscious deep meditation, during which a person was believed to have contact with the spirit world.

tumulus mound of earth or stones, made to mark a burial place.

INDEX